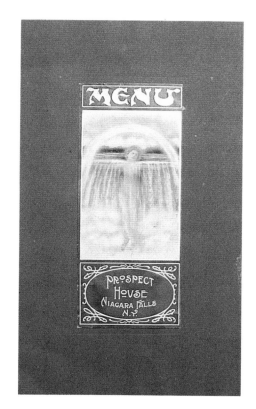

MENU

PROSPECT
HOUSE
NIAGARA FALLS
N.Y.

A LA CARTE

In Shepheard's Hall, Cairo.

M. V. "VULCANIA"
MEDITERRANEAN CRUISE

DINER

CONSOMMÉ AUX PATES D'ITALIE

—

SABOT DE LANGOUSTINE CARDINAL

—

MÉDAILLON DE BOEUF SAUTÉ "DAME NELLY"

—

CHAUD FROID DE VOLAILLE JEANNETTE

SALADE MISS JAFFA

—

ANANAS DIPLOMATE

—

CORBEILLE D'EVE

—

KING DAVID HOTEL
JERUSALEM   Le 15 Mars, 1937

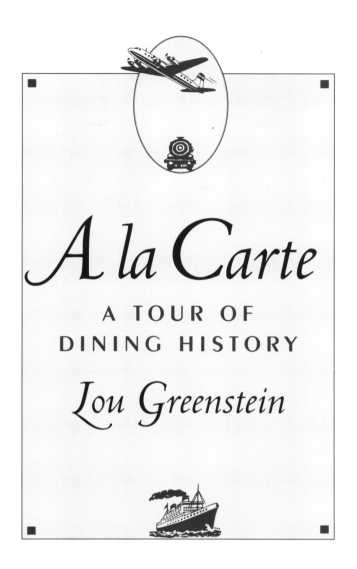

A la Carte

A TOUR OF DINING HISTORY

Lou Greenstein

PBC INTERNATIONAL, INC.

DEDICATION

To my wife Zelma for putting up with all my collections and for being a great working partner.

To my father who will never see this book, thank you for all the restaurants you took me to as a child, and the pride you took in my career.

To my mother who brought the appreciation of art and design into my life.

To my children, Rachel and Joshua, who by their being, give direction to my life.

ACKNOWLEDGMENTS

When I first met Penny Sibal in Chicago, at the 1988 National Restaurant Show, I would never have thought this book was a possibility. Her memory and card file system are truly remarkable.

Thanks to Kevin Clark my Editor, a gentleman, a scholar and friend, without whose help, guidance and patience this book would not have been a reality.

Thanks to Bill McConnell, our photographer extraordinaire, whose back may never recover from a twelve hour photographic shoot.

Thanks to Santo Bordonaro and Ursula Hope for their help with translations.

Thanks to Walter Bilowz for his help in legal matters.

Distributor to the book trade in the United States and Canada:
Rizzoli International Publications Inc.
300 Park Avenue South
New York, NY 10010

Distributor to the art trade in the United States and Canada:
PBC International, Inc.
One School Street
Glen Cove, NY 11542
1-800-527-2826
Fax 516-676-2738

Distributor throughout the rest of the world:
Hearst Books International
1350 Avenue of the Americas
New York, NY 10019

LIBRARY OF CONGRESS CATALOGING-IN-PUBLICATION DATA
Greenstein, Lou.
    A la carte / by Lou Greenstein.
        p.   cm.
    Includes index.
    ISBN 0-86636-184-7
    1. Menus. 2. Menu design. I. Title.
TX911.3.M45G74 1992
642'.5--dc20
                                           92-27132
                                                CIP

CAVEAT—Information in this text is believed accurate, and will pose no problem for the student or casual reader. However, the author was often constrained by information contained in signed release forms, information that could have been in error or not included at all. Any misinformation (or lack of information) is the result of failure in these attestations. The author has done whatever is possible to insure accuracy.

Color separation, printing and binding by
Toppan Printing Co. (H.K.) Ltd. Hong Kong

Design by Beth Tondreau Design
Typography by TypeLink, Inc.

Printed in Hong Kong
10 9 8 7 6 5 4 3 2 1

Contents

RUINES D'ANGKOR-WAT

GRAND HOTEL D'ANGKOR
et HOTEL DES RUINES

DIRECTION
A. MESSNER

Siemréap-Angkor
(CAMBODGE)

Menu

Déjeuner du **IER JUIN 1935**

Œufs au choix sans supplément. — Eggs by choice without extra.

1 — Hors d'Oeuvre Variés

2 — Sauté de volaille Clamart

3 — Aubergines bonne femme

4 — entrecôte garnie

5 — Forestière

6 — Fromage

7 — Corbeille de fruits

8 — Café thé infusions

Café filtre spécial	$ 0.40	Special filter coffee	$ 0.40
Petit Déjeuner	0.80	Early Breakfast	0.80
Breakfast	1.50	Breakfast	1.50
Breakfast avec café ou thé	1.80	Breakfast with coffée or tea	1.80
Déjeuner fourchette de 11 h. à midi	3.00	Luncheon from 11 am. to midi	3.00
Dîner fourchette de 19 h. à 20 h	3.00	Dinner from 7 pm. to 8 pm.	3.00
Service dans les chambres, déjeuner ou dîner	1.00	Meals served in rooms, dinner or lunch an extra charge of	1.00

SUPPLÉMENT

Fromage frais 0.50
Fruits d'Europe ou de Californie.

EXTRAS

Fresh cheese 0.50
European or Californian fruits.

Il est expressément défendu d'introduire des liquides dans l'hôtel. – Toute infraction entraînera, par bouteille, un droit de bouchon.
Pour les eaux minérales . . . . . $ 0.50
Pour les vins de champagne et spiritueux, de $ 1.00 à 5.00

It is expressly forbidden to introduce into the Hotel all liquids. All Breaches of this regulation will entails the charge of "corkage" upon each bottle.
Fir all mineral waters . . . . . $ 0.50
For wine champagnes and Spirits . . . . . from $ 1.00 at 5.00

IMP R. AKKAUR - LYON, PARIS

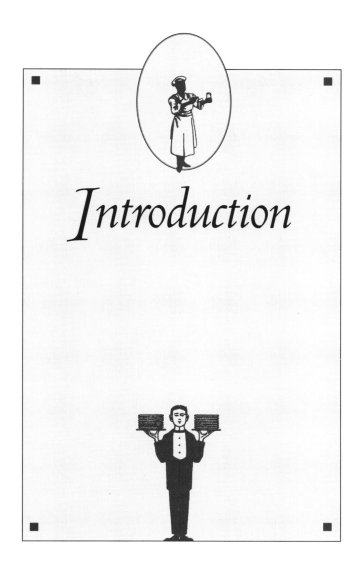

Introduction

$\mathcal{T}$he visually delightful pages of A LA CARTE weave together a new understanding of food and its cultural origins, while serving to all hours of enjoyable reading. Chefs, artists, historians, gourmands, economists, and advertising moguls alike, sitting down with this book of menus, will find their individual palates of interest fully stimulated.

For food historians who enjoy interpreting the beginnings and development of holiday celebrations, these period menus present a delicious offering. For example, history tells us that Valentine's Day celebrations began in the early 1880s. Through menus, we learn how restaurants picked up on this romantic holiday quickly. Independence Day's importance during the 1880s is illustrated through this eclectic collection. Today, the Fourth of July has become a backyard cookout gathering rather than an occasion to eat at restaurants, but over 100 years ago, Independence Day in many parts of the country was more widely celebrated than Christmas. Restaurants created July 4th menus which attracted the customer immediately. The menus trace this change. New information about our culture from holidays to food is found with A LA CARTE's informative and colorful pages.

Regional menu favorites in the days before cross-country trucking, refrigerated trailers, warehouses and frozen concentrates illustrate how we ate what was harvested near the restaurant and hotel. Insights into the popular and seasonal foods of each time period can be gleaned from the selection of foods presented on the menus. Eating corn on the cob in February during a Florida vacation, or navel oranges in California was news to write home about on hand-lithographed, one-cent postcards. Contrast the menus of black bear, squirrel and wild boar to the spa cuisine that is currently popular, or to the menus of today's rapidly growing natural food restaurants. Menus change in response to the customers' needs, lifestyles and tastes, as well as tell a wonderful story about these changes. That is the fascination behind this wonderful collection.

Artistically, this book is a treasure. Commercial artists made these menus distinctive and attractive. Stories of these artists, who worked as commercial artists in order to keep bread on the table, are bountiful. There are certainly many, interesting tales behind the beautiful covers and pages of these menus. Spending time with the artwork on each menu brings you closer to an understanding of the artist and the times. Fanciful and serious, the artwork renders an interpretation of the event or restaurant, as well as an expectation of the wonderful experience ahead for the diner. An analogy to the artwork on these menus would be the jackets of today's books. In both cases, wonderful artistic talent has been applied to attract and delight the reader.

Chefs and restaurant managers will be delighted with Lou Greenstein's work. His budding menu collection was used to recreate special menu items, as well as whole food events for a 600-seat restaurant at

Mystic Seaport. The resource for all these menus was the desire to create historically accurate foods from the 19th century. People responded enthusiastically to these ideas. I expect that this selection of menus will begin to inspire new restaurant experiences throughout America.

These menus have the ability to conjure up memories. Looking at them will inspire readers to recall fond trips on ocean liners, holiday dinners at large hotels, traditional political events, and many other special celebrations.

Whether you are an historian, a student of culture, a chef, a restaurant owner, an artist, or just someone who is filled with wonderful memories of restaurant experiences, you will delight in the way this collection of menus serves you. It has told many wonderful stories to us.

A debt of thanks is owed to Lou Greenstein and his family. He has spent years, and a lot of his own money, to collect and preserve these menus. He did neither for profit, nor to write this book, but out of love for what these menus represent to culinary history and to American history. His collection now numbers in the thousands. This gentleman has provided a great service in preserving an important part of the history of this country over the past two hundred years. This book of menus represents the first publication of Lou Greenstein's collection. I hope many more books will follow that will captivate the reader as much as this one has.

THOMAS H. AAGESON
President
Mystic Seaport Museum Stores

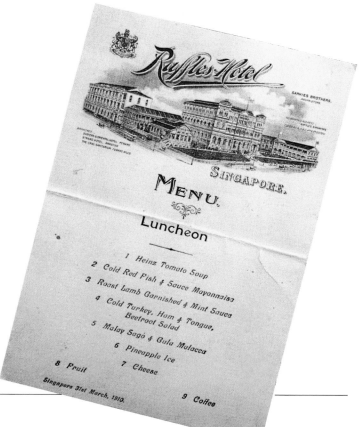

AUF WIEDERSEHEN!

★

ABSCHIEDS-ESSEN
FAREWELL-DINNER

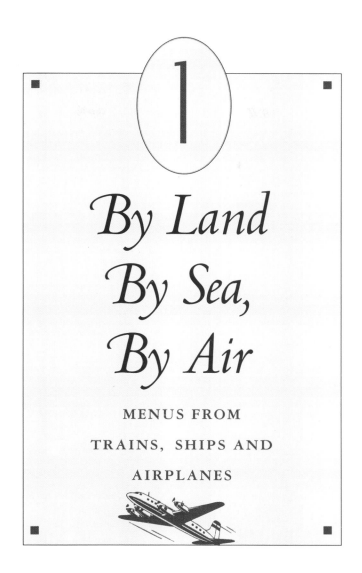

1

By Land By Sea, By Air

MENUS FROM

TRAINS, SHIPS AND

AIRPLANES

*T*here is an old expression that the army travels on its stomach. This expression might just as well apply to everyone that has to go from one place to another. As we developed better ways of moving people, we had to feed them while they were underway. The simple fare of the weigh station became the formal service of the trans-continental dining cars. At each juncture the choices became more and more elaborate. The longer you were involved in travel the better and more extensive the menu had to be.

NEW YORK CENTRAL RAILROAD

Breakfast
The Lake Shore Limited—New York to Chicago
March 26, 1903

This menu is very stylish and offered a complete breakfast with everything you could ever want in the morning. The meal included steaks, poultry, fresh fruits and pure bottled water. Since this was a twenty-four hour train, a full liquor list appears.

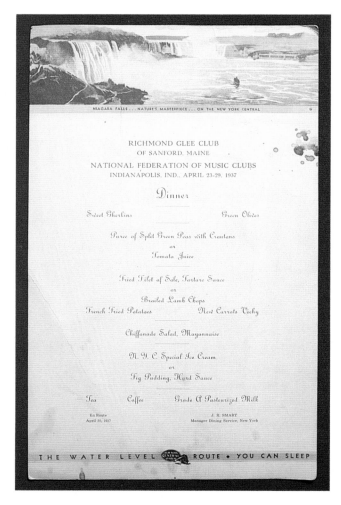

NEW YORK CENTRAL SYSTEM

Dinner
En Route to Indianapolis, Indiana
April 30, 1937

A single page bill of fare menu was designed for a traveling group; this was a sleeper train.

SOUTHERN PACIFIC LINES

Dinner
En Route to San Francisco National
Federation of Music Clubs
June 20, 1931

This is a beautiful cover showing the high quality of service with an image of the old mission trails at the top of the window.

SOUTHERN PACIFIC RAILWAY

Breakfast & Dinner
En Route to the 1939 Golden Gate
International Exposition
August, 1939

The images on the front of the menus are of the Golden Gate Exposition. Prices for breakfast range from fifty cents to a dollar, for steak with eggs. Prices for dinner range from ninety cents to a dollar seventy-five for the special.

CANADIAN PACIFIC RAILWAY

Dining Car Service
Lunch and Dinner Menus
Somewhere En Route
1939

Like a ship, each train had a name; one of the menus shown came from the *Dominion* while the other from the *Mountaineer*. The Canadian Pacific Line also operated hotels; the pictured Chateau Frontenac was one of them.

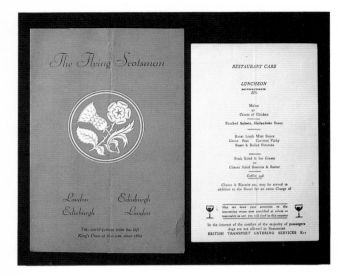

BRITISH TRANSPORT CATERING SERVICES

The Flying Scotsman
Breakfast and Lunch Menus
1940s

This historic train menu was a classic of its time. This train traveled from London to Edinburgh every day at 10:00 AM, then returned. They served morning coffee, luncheon and afternoon tea. The color is wedgewood blue with a white emblem, referring to the china pattern colors used exclusively on this train.

NEW YORK CENTRAL SYSTEM

War Time Dining Car Service
Luncheon
En Route to Chicago
1943

This menu describes the many rules for war time dining. It requests preference be given to military personnel with a ten percent reduction in food cost. The cover is a picture of Chicago's North Michigan Boulevard.

THE NEW HAVEN RAILROAD

Special Luncheon Menu
En Route, Boston to New York
June, 1940

This menu is full of advertising for theater, shopping and hotels and contains six pages with a two page activity insert that was changed monthly. In June of that year, you could see Olsen and Johnson's "Hellzapoppin" at the Wintergarten for $1.10. It cost $3.30 for the best seats. (*Opposite*).

menu

SPECIAL LUNCHEON

New Haven Railroad

PENNSYLVANIA RAILROAD

"Train Talks"
Mile-A-Minute Meals
January, 1938

This little pamphlet is a study of the Pennsylvania Railway system dining car service. It has diagrams of the kitchen car and the full dining system, and supplies some interesting statistics about their patrons' consumption per year: 2,500,000 eggs, 1,300,000 oranges, 550,000 pounds of fowl, 390,000 pounds of beef, 490,000 pounds of pork, 1,000,000 pounds of potatoes, and 2,000,000 cups of coffee. (*Opposite*).

SOUTHERN PACIFIC

Children's Menu
En Route
September, 1939

This four page menu explains all the jobs aboard the train and tells a little story about each worker. It also tells where all the food for the dining car comes from.

Train Talks

Informal discussions by the Pennsylvania Railroad with its patrons on matters of mutual interest and concern.

JANUARY, 1938

Mile-a-Minute Meals

Behind the Scenes in the Dining Car Service of a Great Railroad

ONE of the many things "taken for granted" on railroads is getting a first rate meal on a speeding train.

* * * *

Your "Limited" has been clicking off a mile a minute or more, and the afternoon slips by. You step from coach or Pullman into a perfectly appointed, air-conditioned, travelling restaurant, and in an atmosphere of inviting leisure enjoy a dinner of your own choosing. It is as attractively prepared, as well cooked, and as deftly served as in an excellent hotel.

For you nothing could be simpler or more casual. Custom has made this service so matter of course that prob-

THE AIRLINES

As planes began flying greater distances, they became larger and more comfortable to accommodate an ever-increasing passenger load. The early boxed lunch flights no longer would fill the need of the customer. The age of dining in the air began for real in the 1950s, and the following menus are a few of the early entries.

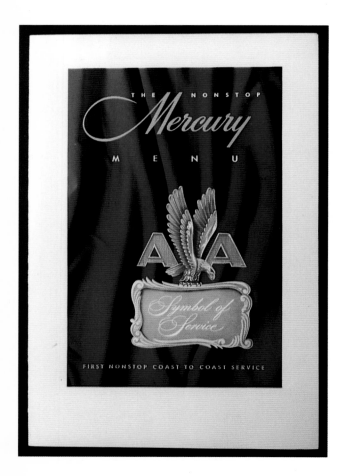

AMERICAN AIRLINES

The Royal Coachman
New York to Fort Worth, Texas
April, 1958

On the back of this menu/postcard, the guest wrote that he had a great meal.

AMERICAN AIRLINES MERCURY MENU

Eight hours coast to coast
Circa 1953

Steak and shrimp were the highlights of this menu, while the back shows the history of coast-to-coast flight. This menu also doubles as a souvenir mailer and comes with an airmail envelope.

PAN AMERICAN AIRLINES

Japan to USA Flight
Circa 1960

This was a special flight, as the menu was printed in French with English titles to impart an elegant air.

UNITED AIRLINES

Mainliner Stratocruisers
Los Angeles to Hawaii
Circa 1957

The back of this menu is a postcard; it was never mailed.

South Pacific

THE SEA

We have come a long way from hard tack and salted meat as the mainstay aboard long sea voyages. The menu of the cruise ship is an art form unto itself. The great ships with names like the *Empress of India, The Queen Mary, The United States* and *The Bremen* were like cities at sea. Since the late 1800s, the food quality aboard these ships has been amazing. The menus that follow are but a few. Some of these menus are from *The Queen Mary,* whose sole purpose was to carry passengers; others are from steamships whose primary purpose was cargo transport. Some steamers carried as few as 10 or 15 passengers while others may have had accommodations for up to 200.

THE SHIP *HOPE*
Dinner
En Route, Destination Unknown
May 16, 1898

This menu, designed from a playing card speaks for itself. It may have been used at a special events dinner.

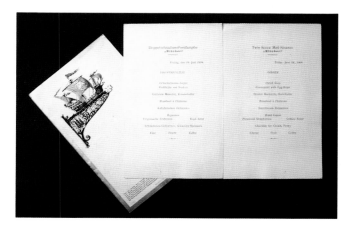

THE TWIN SCREW MAIL STEAMER
BLUCHER—HAMBURG-AMERICA LINE

Dinner
En Route, Destination Unknown
June 23, 1909

This ship's menu is printed in German and English. The fare was not elaborate, as this was a working steamer rather than a cruise ship.

S.S. CEDRIC: EUROPA-COLUMBIA LINE

En Route, Destination Unknown
October 2, 1913

This is an example of another steamer menu with a more elaborate design.

R.M.S. OCEANIC: WHITE STAR LINE

En Route, Destination Unknown
November 4 & 5, 1913

These menus form a bridge over the Atlantic; one pictures the Statue of Liberty, while the other pictures scenes of London.

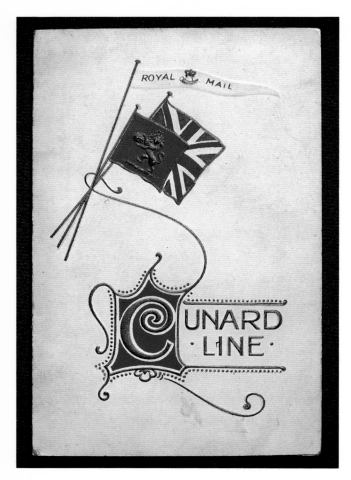

TWIN SCREW MAIL STEAMER *DRESDEN*: NORDDEUTSCHER LLOYD BREMEN

Bremen-Cherborg-Queenstown-New York
August 15, 1929

This grouping represents a complete ship's kit that includes the menu jacket holder, a complete passenger list, instruction manual, a series of menus from each day, and the farewell dinner menu. Each item is written in German and English. The menus are well-written and represent an extremely high level of culinary skill.

R.M.S. AQUITANIA: CUNARD LINE

En Route, London to New York
July 19, 1919

This was a royal mail ship that also transported passengers. This particular menu was created to celebrate British Peace Day.

S.S. HAMBURG: HAMBURG-AMERICAN LINE

En Route to New York
September 1, 1930

This menu celebrates the "Winky Dinner." Each course is named for a character in literature, and is described in flowing, flowery verse.

AMERICAN TWIN SCREW STEAMSHIP, S.S. REPUBLIC: UNITED STATES LINE

New York-Queenstown-Plymouth-Cherbourg-Bremen
July 4, 1929

This grouping represents a complete ship's record of passage which includes the menu jacket holder, a complete passenger list, instruction manual, a series of menus from each day and the farewell dinner menu. The menu for breakfast and lunch are single card, bill of fare style, and the dinner menus are a simple, folded jacket. The food is very American with a few German specials like pigs' knuckles and sauerkraut, included to satisfy German guests. The ship was captained by Commander A.M. Moore, U.S.N.R.

S.S. MUNGARO: MUNSON STEAMSHIP LINES

Dinner D'Adieu
New York-Miami-Nassau N.P.-Habana (Havana)
October 4, 1934

The ship departed Saturday, September 22, 1934 and arrived on October 5, 1934. The menu also has a complete list of cruise passengers as additional pages.

R.M.S. VOLDENDAM: HOLLAND-AMERICA LINE

Tourist Class Get-Together Dinner
June 26, 1932

These menus are a lot less fancy than First Class, and reflect a slightly different, more unencumbered food style.

S.S. ILE-DE-FRANCE: FRENCH LINE

Transatlantic Cruise
October 13, 1935

This is one of those classic menus; the French lines were known for their outstanding cuisine. The menu was presented in French and English; luncheon menu has twice the choices of the average cruise dinner menu. All of the menus were printed in France.

Q.T.E.V. MONARCH OF BERMUDA: FURNESS BERMUDA LINE

En Route, New York to Bermuda
January, 1935

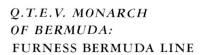

The *Monarch* offered a very advanced menu for the period. They prepared a complete vegetarian menu for each meal along with all the traditional items. The menu is also a playbill for the day and evening entertainment.

R.M.S. FRANCONIA: CUNARD LINES &
CUNARD WHITE STAR LINES

Auld Lang Syne Farewell Menus
1933 and 1936

These two menus reflect the shipping line's name change, but the menu designer A.T. McDonald remained the same. The mermaid toasting Puck is the 1936 version.

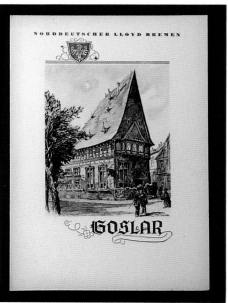

S.S. EUROPA: NORDDEUTSCHER LLOYD BREMEN

August 17-22, 1937

Six menus representing a series of 20 from a single crossing are shown. The selection includes the welcome and farewell menus; this was a first-class crossing.

1857 H.H.Meier 1888   1857 E.Crüsemann 1869

80 Jahre NORDDEUTSCHER LLOYD BREMEN 1857–1937

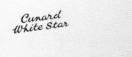

R.M.S. LACONIA: CUNARD WHITE STAR LINES

Luncheon Menu Covers
June, 1937

This collection of six menus represents the day-to-day menu variety aboard the *Laconia* for a given week.

S.S. EUROPA: NORDDEUTSCHER LLOYD BREMEN

Jubilee Dinner
Atlantic Passage Tourist Class
June 23, 1937

This menu represents the 80 year anniversary of the Bremen lines. The two portraits on the front of the menu jacket are the founders, and printed on the back page of the jacket is the history of the shipping line. The dinner was very impressive, even in tourist class. (*Opposite*).

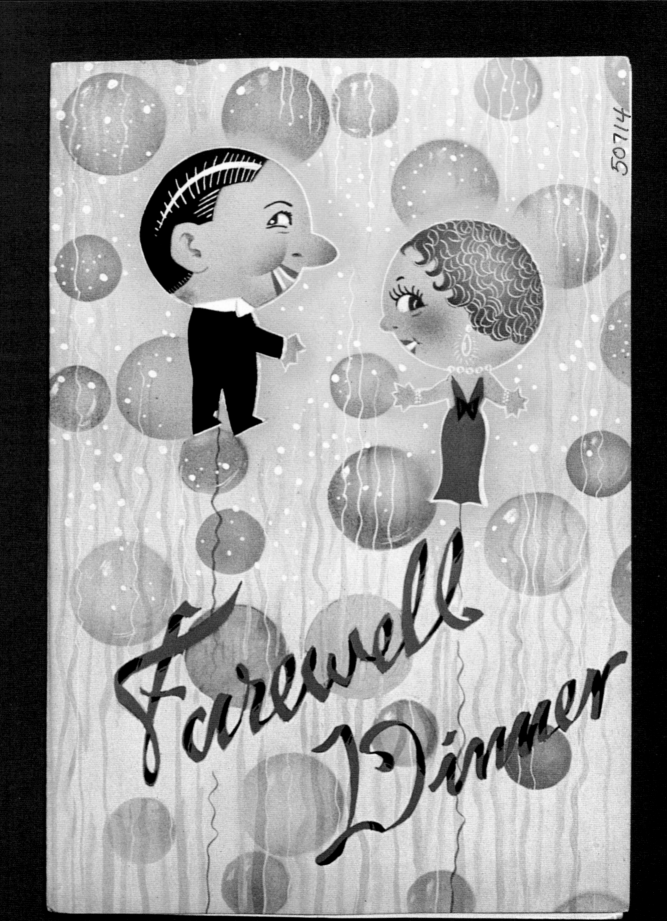

Farewell Dinner

EASTERN STEAMSHIP LINER

Breakfast Menu
Circa 1940s

This company advertised ten coastwide services. Note the early bridge design and classic cars. A highlighted item worth noting is their "Club Meals."

R.M.S. VOLENDAM: HOLLAND-AMERICA LINE

Farewell Dinner
En Route to New York, Tourist Class
July 25, 1937

This menu, although very pretty on the outside, lists a very uninteresting Farewell Dinner. Only two choices for dinner are shown, fillets of mackerel or roast duckling, and only one choice in each of the other courses. Dessert was "farewell" cake. (*Opposite*).

S.S. PRINCESS ALICE: CANADIAN PACIFIC B.C. COAST STEAMSHIPS

Farewell Dinner
Summer Cruise to Alaska
Date Unknown

The menu poetically commemorates the land of the Aurora, with a poem by Robert W. Service and offers a rather unusual fish course, Chicken Halibut Cheeks.

S.S. URUGUAY: MOORE-McCORMACK LINES

Dinner Menus
En Route to South America
June, 1948

Each of these menus represents a country: the cover titled "Rolling A Cigar" represents Paraguay, and the cover titled "Dancing The Gato" represents Argentina. Both Covers were designed and illustrated by Ada Peacock.

S.S. BRAZIL: MOORE-McCORMACK LINES

Dinner Menu
New York to South America
Friday, July 25, 1941

Also known as the good neighbor fleet, the Moore-McCormack lines primarily serviced South America. The cover of this menu is just wonderful with its exotic illustration and brilliant coloring.

R.M.S. NIEUW AMSTERDAM: HOLLAND-AMERICA LINE

South American Cruise
January-February, 1949

This set of ten menus represents a cross section of the menu styles for an extended period cruise (notice the complete change of design for each week). The assortment includes breakfast, lunch and dinner with a copy of the farewell banquet menu.

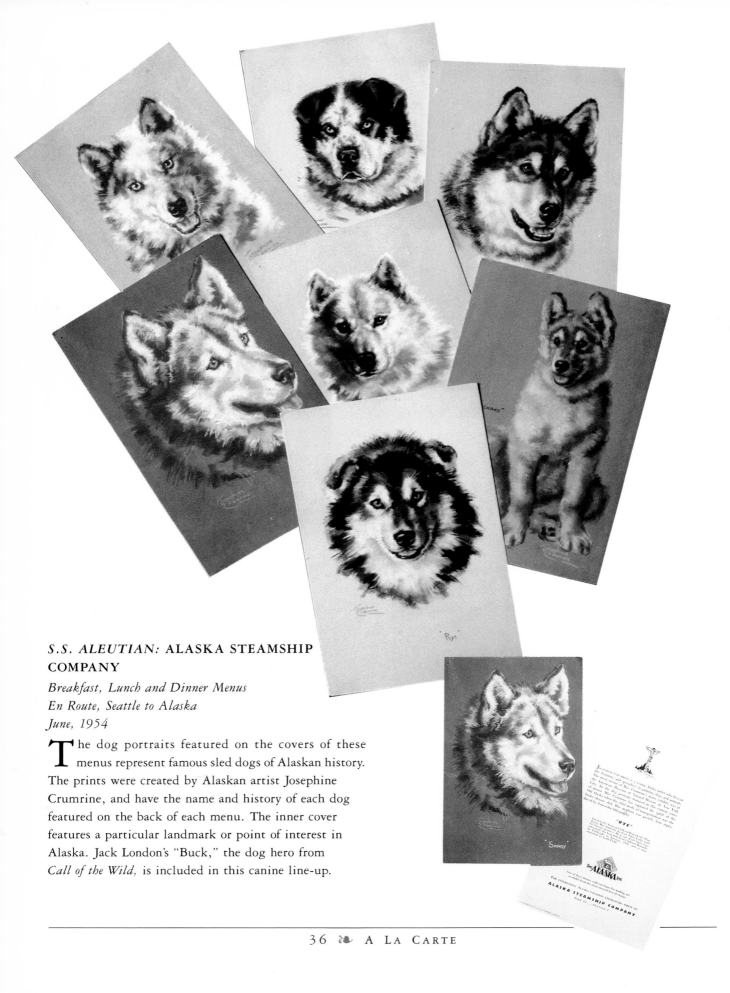

S.S. ALEUTIAN: ALASKA STEAMSHIP COMPANY

Breakfast, Lunch and Dinner Menus
En Route, Seattle to Alaska
June, 1954

The dog portraits featured on the covers of these menus represent famous sled dogs of Alaskan history. The prints were created by Alaskan artist Josephine Crumrine, and have the name and history of each dog featured on the back of each menu. The inner cover features a particular landmark or point of interest in Alaska. Jack London's "Buck," the dog hero from *Call of the Wild,* is included in this canine line-up.

EMPRESS OF BRITAIN: CANADIAN PACIFIC STEAMSHIP LINES

Liverpool-Greenock-Quebec-Montreal
September 1959

These two menus represent the gala dinner and the Au Revoir Dinner of this transatlantic crossing. The Au Revoir menu features an abstract of the ship's log which indicated that there were very heavy seas during the entire crossing. The ship sailed September 18th and arrived September 25th.

S.S. UNITED STATES: UNITED STATES LINES

Breakfast Menu
Transatlantic Crossing
November, 1959

S.S. UNITED STATES:
UNITED STATES LINES

Lunch and Dinner Menus
Transatlantic Crossing
November, 1959

The *S.S. United States* was the flagship of the United States Lines; the cuisine aboard this ship was outstanding. The menu with the print of the *S.S. United States* on the cover was the gala dinner menu. Each dinner menu had on its inner cover a foldout featuring one of the specially commissioned works of art that adorned the ship's dining rooms and lounges. This was one of the few places in the world where you would find Mexican Shark's Tail soup and Kangaroo Tail En Tasse in the evening's soup selection (November 6, 1959).

LUNCHEON

UNITED STATES LINES

DU JOUR

...or Frais Frappé

Suprême de Fruits

Huîtres de Blue Point

Céleri en Branche

Potage aux Nageoires de Requin

... à la Parisienne

...hasseur

...s à la Hoover

...ce Béarnaise

Pommes Fondantes

...line

Petits Fours

...vers

...ruits

The sea was the inspiration
for the two panels by
Raymond Wendell in the
observation lounge
of the UNITED STATES.
Extensive research preceded
the painting of the
Atlantic Ocean floor,
which occupies the port
side alcove, and the
prevailing currents,
which are represented
on the star-board
panel. Topographical
features show through the
surface patterns.

...TED STATES"

...ANDERSON
...R

...Minutes Tonight

HORS-D'ŒUVRE	Blue Point Oysters on the Half Shell Fresh California Fruit Cup au Kirsch
	Chilled Spanish Melon Pickled Walnuts Artichoke à la Grecque
	Astrakhan Malossol Caviar on Ice Smoked Irish Salmon or Sturgeon
	Salad à la Reine Iced Table Celery Queen and Ripe Olives
	Pâté de Foie Gras Royans Mushrooms, Françoise
	Fresh Crabmeat Cocktail Egg à la Russe
SOUPS	Cream of Mushrooms Mexican Shark Fins Bouillabaisse Merseillaise
FISH	Kangaroo Tail en Tasse **Cold:** Consommé, Madrilène Vichyssoise
	Boiled Fresh Brook Trout, Melted Butter, Creamed Horseradish
	Fried Digby Boy Scallops, Sauce Tartare, Cole Slow
COLD BUFFET	Dover Sole, Sauté Meunière, Potato Salad
	Westfalian Ham, Asparagus, Vinaigrette Gefillte Fish, Chrain in Aspic
ENTRÉES	Roast Chicken and Baked Virginia Ham, Asparagus Salad
	Smoked Breast of Gosling
	Coquille Saint-Jacques à la Parisienne
ROASTS	Braised Smoked Ox-Tongue, Florentine Swiss Rarebit
	Légume: Braunschweiger Asparagus, Sauce Hollandaise
	Long Island Duckling, Apple and Prune Stuffing, Giblet Sauce
	Prime Rib of Beef au Jus, Rasped Horseradish
COMPOTES	Leg and Saddle of Lamb, English Mint Sauce
	Fresh Jersey Ham, Mirepoix, Apple Sauce
FROM THE GRILL	Peaches Kumquats Bartlett Pears Cherries Mixed
(10 TO 15 MINUTES)	Tenderloin Steak, Sauce Béarnaise
VEGETABLES	Bitokes à la Russe, Risotto, Sour Cream Sauce French Lamb Chops on Toast
POTATOES	Carrots, Vichy Braised Red Cabbage Spinach, Naturel Fresh Broccoli
SALADS	Haricots Verts Risotto Cauliflower Chanterelles, Sauté Wax Beans
	Boiled New Mashed Baked Idaho Between the Act Candied Sweet
CHEESE	Boston Lettuce Sliced Tomato Endive Chicory Fruit Knob Celery
	Dressings: French Thousand Island Special Garlic Russian
DESSERTS	Young American, Stilton, Swiss, Edam, Gruyère, Boursin, Tilsiter or Brie
	Cherry Tart with Whipped Cream Macedoine of Fruits in Wine Jelly
	Petits Fours Meringue Glacée au Chocolat Lemon Sherbet
	Nougat Parfait Frangipan Biscuit Tortoni
	Vanilla or Strawberry Ice Cream, Wafers
	Fresh Fruit Basket Grapes on Ice
	Coffee: American Sanka Mocha Kaffee Hag
	Teas: Orange Pekoe Mint English Breakfast Green

LS—FCD-1

Demi Tasse is served in the Smoking Room and Cocktail Lounge after Dinner

Friday, November 6, 1959

GRAND
HÔTEL

Bruxelles

LITH. F. APPEL PARIS.

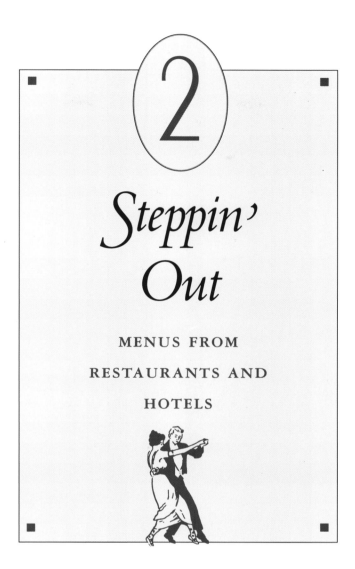

2

Steppin' Out

MENUS FROM RESTAURANTS AND HOTELS

*W*hat must have begun as a spoken list of the day's fare in small wayside inns, has become a chronicle of great historical and cultural significance. The spoken food offerings that evolved to the written art form shown here, help identify the regional bounty that existed historically. With the growth of the railway and highway systems, special foods available only in certain areas were able to be shipped to new frontiers.

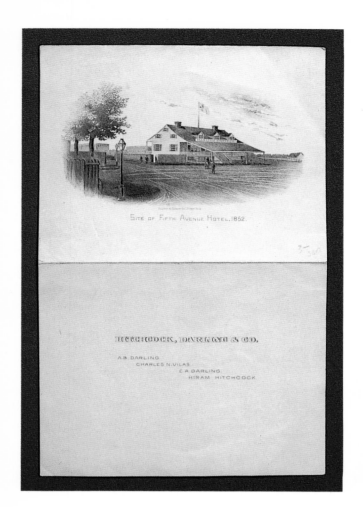

FIFTH AVENUE HOTEL
(MADISON COTTAGES)

New York, New York
1852

The cover of this breakfast menu shows an engraving of this early wayside stop. The property was managed by Hitchcock, Darling & Co.

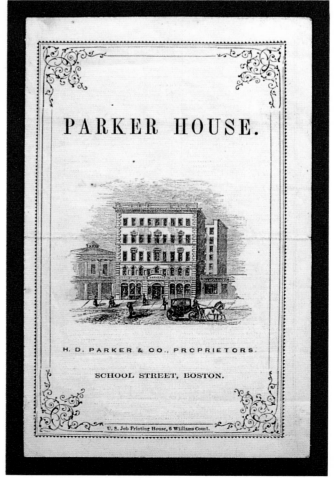

THE PARKER HOUSE

Boston, Massachusetts
Dinner
Tuesday, June 12, 1860

The cover pictures an engraving of the original hotel, while the back lists a superb period wine and liquor offering. At the bottom of the menu is the request "Gentlemen are particularly requested not to fee the waiters; as they are paid by the proprietors."

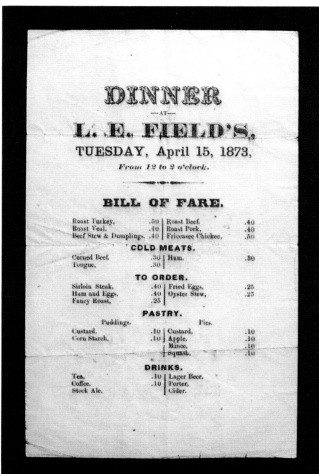

L.E. FIELD'S

Dinner
April 15, 1873

This represents a simple, bill of fare menu. The location is unknown.

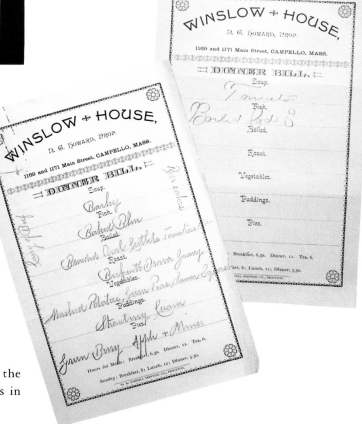

WINSLOW HOUSE

Campello, Massachusetts
Date Unknown

These two menus represent an alternative to the printed daily menu. Here, the proprietor writes in the items that were available at the market.

ROCKINGHAM HOUSE,

PORTSMOUTH, N. H.

W. HILTON, - PROPRIETOR.

THE ROCKINGHAM HOUSE

Portsmouth, New Hampshire
1880

These are two menus from the hotel, recycled from the Wentworth House, Newcastle, New Hampshire. The hotels were by F. W. Hilton & Co.

YOUNG'S HOTEL

Boston, Massachusetts
Dinner
Sunday, June 12, 1881

This cover was created by John A. Lowell & Co. Engravers and printed by Alfred Mudge & Sons, for Hall & Whipple, the hotel proprietors. It advertises a special 5 o'clock dinner, and lists six regional varieties of oysters served in sixteen different styles.

MASCONOMO HOUSE

Manchester (by the sea), Massachusetts
Dinner
August 31, 1881

These menu covers were part of a series designed and printed by the William H. Brett Engraving Company of Boston, with a map of the region on the back cover.

UNITED STATES HOTEL

Saratoga Springs, New York
Circa 1880s

Pictured are a breakfast and dinner menu from this classic spa. The back of the menu depicts a magnificent lawn view of the hotel and features separate dining hours for children and servants. It also states that should a child occupy a seat at a public table, full price would be charged. (*Opposite*).

GRAND HOTEL BRUXELLES

Paris, France
Dinner
May 16, 1882

This small cardboard bill of fare contains a handwritten menu.

MANHATTAN BEACH HOTEL

New York, New York
Carte du Jour
July 25, 1883

The cover of this menu pictures four hotels operated by James H. Breslin. Two are summer resorts or spas, two are city hotels. The engravings are by Dempsey & Carroll, while the printing is by Busey and Rooney.

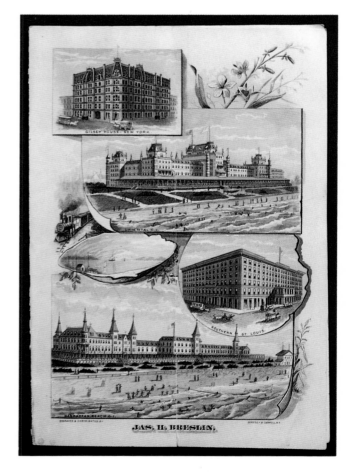

OCEAN BLUFF HOTEL

Kennebunkport, Maine
Dinner
July 20, 1888; August 20 and 24, 1888; and July 11
and 20, 1889

This collection of dinner menus was created by Robinson Engraving Company in Boston, Massachusetts. Each is numbered and the interiors feature the dinner fare and a view of the hotel. (*Opposite*).

PABST HOTEL

Milwaukee, Wisconsin
Dinner
July 25, 1892

This menu reflects the bounty of the region. For example, the main courses are smoked jowl with spinach and loin of antelope, served with a sour cream sauce. Guests having friends to meals were requested to leave notice at the office or report to the head waiter. G.W. Porth was the manager of this establishment.

WEST HOTEL

Minneapolis, Minnesota
Dinner
June 25, 1893

This lovely menu cover was designed by William L. Banning Jr. of St. Paul, Minnesota. All water used in the hotel came from its own artesian wells. Additionally, 11 varieties of bottled mineral water were featured on the menu. It was suggested, "by applying at the office, guests can procure fine carriages and livery at reasonable rates and thus avoid extortionate charges from irresponsible parties." The proprietors were Geebamen & Murphy.

BAILEY'S HOTEL

London, S.W.
Breakfast
June 21, 1911

Part of a group managed by Empire Hotels, the Bailey was considered to be one of the leading hotels in London. (*Opposite*).

GREENS-PARK HOTEL

Dublin, Ireland
May 27, 1902

This menu design was part of a series titled "Glimpses of the Celestial Empire." This particular menu "The Empress in Her Garden" is handwritten. The back contains a Chinese doctor's prescription: "Powdered snakes, 2 parts; wasps and their nests, 1 part; centipedes, 6 parts; scorpions, 4 parts; toads, 20 parts; grind thoroughly, mix with honey, and make into small pills. Two to be taken four times a day."

RAFFLES HOTEL

Singapore
Luncheon
March 31, 1910

The first course is listed as canned Heinz Tomato Soup, obviously a delicacy for this five-star hotel!

Menu

Empire Hotels

BAILEY'S HOTEL,
LONDON, S.W.

EXPECTATION

Menu

EVENING MEAL

Bouillon, en Tasse

Broiled Halibut, Maître d'Hotel
Cucumbers   Olives

Grilled Tenderloin Steak, Sauce, Green Peas
Loin of Spring Lamb, Sauce Bordalaise
                            Fried Sweet Potatoes
Baked Potatoes   Lima Beans   Force
Hominy   EGGS   Poached
            Fried   Scrambled
Boiled   OMELETS
            Spanish, Ham and Plain
                    COLD
Roast Beef   Ham   Lamb Tongues   Sardines   Veal
    Pigs' Feet   Corned Beef   Lamb   Chicken
    CHICKEN MAYONNAISE   DRESSED LETTUCE
    Cream Tartar Biscuits   Hermits
        Assorted Cake   Raspberries
        Preserved Peaches
    Tea   Coffee   Cocoa   M
        Fabyan House, August 6, 190

Fabyan House
White Mountains, N. H.
O. G. BARRON, Mgr.

PROSPECT HOUSE

Niagara Falls, New York
Circa 1910

If you look closely at this menu cover design, the famous "Maid of the Mist" is barely visible. The back cover depicts an Indian grinding corn, and invites hotel guests to visit the Natural Food Company, and watch the manufacture of shredded whole wheat biscuits. This company later became known as Nabisco.

MURRAY'S APARTMENTS

New York, New York
Supper
1910

The back of the menu advertises "Murray's Apartments. They include a parlor, bedroom, tiled bath and shower. Every apartment is furnished, as a man of refined taste would furnish his own home. Rates $2.50 a day and upwards. Ask for the wine list."

FABYAN HOUSE

White Mountains, New Hampshire
July 30, August 6, and September 17, 1905

This selection of menus represents different jacket designs used by the hotel for different meals. Some of the menu items include Enoch's pickles and roast tame duck, stuffed. The hotel manager was O.G. Barron. *(Opposite).*

AMERICAN BAR.

SKINDLES HOTEL,
MAIDENHEAD BRIDGE.

COCKTAILS.

SKINDLES HOTEL

Maidenhead Bridge, England
May, 1925

This is the menu for the American Bar at Skindles. All prices are in pounds and the list offers such classics as the Palmetto, the Hoola Hoola, the Zaza, the Silver Streak, the Merry Widow, and the Pussyfoot. The British choices included such staid items as the Royal Clover Cup, Sherry Cobbler, and the Night Cap.

KIERAN J. LOWRY,
Manager

ELKS HOTEL ROOF GARDEN
OPENING NIGHT
Fall and Winter Season
PRESENTING
Joe Rines and his Famous Broadcasting Orchester and Revue

ELKS HOTEL ROOF GARDEN

Boston, Massachusetts
Fall and Winter Season, 1925

This menu acts as an evening's program as well. A few of the acts were Agnes Ryan, "The Roof Garden Song Bird;" Clair Nolan, "The Fuzzie Fuzzie Girl In a Cake Walk;" and Lamkin and LaCroix, "The Merry Prancers."

HOTEL METROPOLE

London, England
Supper
April 29, 1927

This is the play bill and supper menu from the show called "The Midnight Follies." The review included the famous American dancers, Rosita and Ramone, in their first London appearance. Supper was very expensive, and offered only the best champagne and foods.

SEVILLA BILTMORE

Habana (Havana), Cuba
Dinner
March 30, 1930

The inner section features a picture of the Maine monument with original guns and anchor chains. The menu also invites guests to purchase cigars at factory prices in the hotel store, and it suggests visitors read, *When It's Cocktail Time In Cuba,* by Basil Woon.

VISTA OF THE ROYAL HAWAIIAN HOTEL FROM THE TROPICAL GARDEN—Photo by Pan

SUNSET FROM WAIKIKI BEACH—By D. de Kisarvay

ROYAL HAWAIIAN HOTEL

Honolulu, Hawaii
March 22, 1931

These seven menu covers were all from the luncheon meal. The cover designs are reproductions of paintings and photos of Honolulu's flowers, gardens and magnificent vistas. The menu offers Parker Ranch Sirloin Steak, Curried Makapu Point Turtle, Poi Cocktail and Native Fish served in Ti leaves. All the eggs, cream and milk were supplied from the hotel's own ranch and dairy. The air temperature that day was 75 degrees and the sea temperature was 77 degrees. (*Opposite*).

GRAND HOTEL D'ANGKOR ET HOTEL DES RUINES

Siemreap-Angkor, Cambodia
Luncheon
June, 1935

English and French were the primary languages spoken, and the menu listed a number of regulations, including, "It is expressly forbidden to introduce into the hotel all liquids. All breaches of this regulation will entail the charge of corkage upon each bottle."

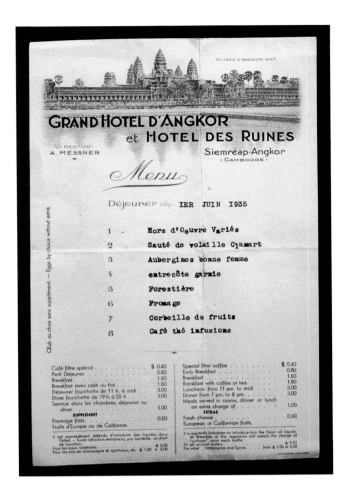

HOTEL DUNAPALOTA (THE RITZ)

Budapest, Hungary
August 23, 1936

This cover is a map of Hungary, and details the distance from Budapest to other major European cities, with a mileage key written in French.

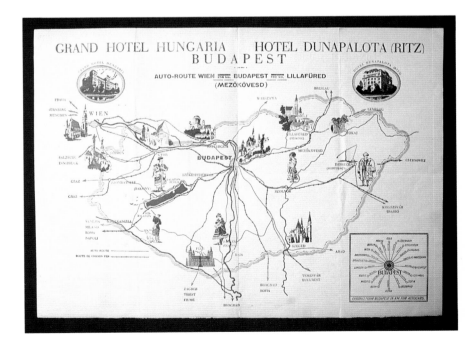

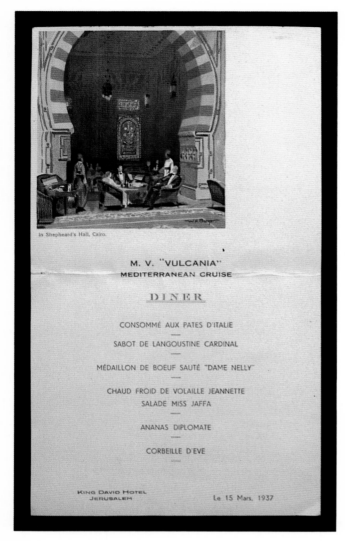

In Shepheard's Hall, Cairo.

M. V. "VULCANIA"
MEDITERRANEAN CRUISE

DINER

CONSOMMÉ AUX PATES D'ITALIE
—
SABOT DE LANGOUSTINE CARDINAL
—
MÉDAILLON DE BOEUF SAUTÉ "DAME NELLY"
—
CHAUD FROID DE VOLAILLE JEANNETTE
SALADE MISS JAFFA
—
ANANAS DIPLOMATE
—
CORBEILLE D'EVE

KING DAVID HOTEL
JERUSALEM   Le 15 Mars, 1937

HOTEL ST. FRANCIS

San Francisco, California
Dinner
August 23, 1939

This extravagant menu is from the mural room at the St. Francis. An interesting point was their escalating cover charge: no charge before 9:00 PM, 75 cents thereafter, and $1.00 on Saturdays. It is quite obvious they did a late night dinner business.

KING DAVID HOTEL

Jerusalem, Israel
Dinner
March 15, 1947

This was a special dinner prepared for the passengers of the *M.V. Vulcania* on her Mediterranean cruise.

HOTEL GENEVE

Mexico City, Mexico
Dinner
November 22, 1938

This menu is rather interesting as it pictures a variety of Mexican culinary utensils and was specially designed for the hotel's American guests.

HOTEL GENEVE
7A. DE LONDRES 130
MEXICO CITY
MEXICO

MENÚ

Nov. 22, 1938

TABLE D'HOTE DINNER $3.50 MEXICAN CY.

FOR WINES & COCKTAILS ASK FOR SEPARATE LIST BASKET LUNCHES FOR MORNING TRIPS MUST BE ORDERED BY ONE P.M. PREVIOUS DAY

Gumbo Soup .... .60

Grapefruit Juice .... .60
or Hors D'oeuvre .... .60

Roast Breast of Chicken 1.50
or Butter Fried Chicken 1.50
or Cold Turkey Plate 1.50
or Grilled T-Bone Steak 1.50
    Baked Sweet Potato
    Buttered Green Peas
    Spiced Apple
    Orange Marmalade Muffin

Cheese Stuffed Celery Sticks & Olives .... .50

Strawberry Ice Cream & Cake .... .60
or Chocolate Ice Box Cake .... .50
or Prune Chiffon Pie .... .50
or Peppermint Mousse, Chocolate Sauce .50
or Fresh Raspberries & Cream .... .50
or Bulgarian Milk .... .30

Tea or Coffee .... .40
Bread & Butter .... .25

BEER? IN MEXICO IT IS—

CERVEZA CARTA BLANCA EXQUISITA

Mexican Culinary Utensils

PLEASE PAY DINING ROOM CASHIER

THE AWAHNEE

Yosemite National Park, California
August 1939 and August 1948

This series of menus was used each year at the park. The covers were reproductions of photographs of Yosemite, by the world-renowned photographer Ansel Adams.

CAMP CURRY

Yosemite National Park, California
August, 1939

This series of menus was used at one of the smaller outing areas of the park and represents breakfast, lunch and dinner. The scenes are of points of interest found in the park.

BANFF SPRINGS HOTEL
Canadian Rockies

Banff Springs Hotel
in the – Canadian Rockies

Canadian Pacific

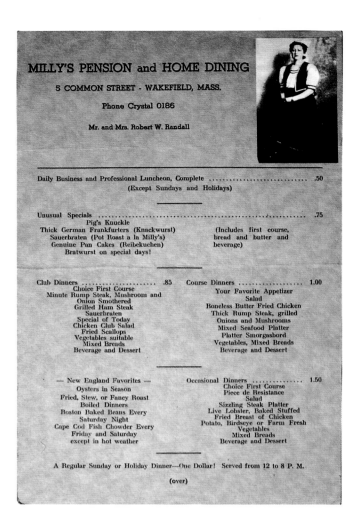

MILLY'S PENSION and HOME DINING

5 COMMON STREET - WAKEFIELD, MASS.

Phone Crystal 0186

Mr. and Mrs. Robert W. Randall

Daily Business and Professional Luncheon, Complete .... .50
(Except Sundays and Holidays)

Unusual Specials .... .75
Pig's Knuckle
Thick German Frankfurters (Knackwurst)   (Includes first course,
Sauerbraten (Pot Roast a la Milly's)   bread and butter and
Genuine Pan Cakes (Reibekuchen)   beverage)
Bratwurst on special days!

Club Dinners .... .85   Course Dinners 1.00
Choice First Course   Your Favorite Appetizer
Minute Rump Steak, Mushroom and   Salad
Onion Smothered   Boneless Butter Fried Chicken
Grilled Ham Steak   Thick Rump Steak, grilled
Sauerbraten   Onions and Mushrooms
Special of Today   Mixed Seafood Platter
Chicken Club Salad   Platter Smorgasbord
Fried Scallops   Vegetables, Mixed Breads
Vegetables suitable   Beverage and Dessert
Mixed Breads
Beverage and Dessert

— New England Favorites —   Occasional Dinners 1.50
Oysters in Season   Choice First Course
Fried, Stew, or Fancy Roast   Piece de Resistance
Boiled Dinners   Salad
Boston Baked Beans Every   Sizzling Steak Platter
Saturday Night   Live Lobster, Baked Stuffed
Cape Cod Fish Chowder Every   Fried Breast of Chicken
Friday and Saturday   Potato, Birdseye or Farm Fresh
except in hot weather   Vegetables
                                      Mixed Breads
                                      Beverage and Dessert

A Regular Sunday or Holiday Dinner—One Dollar! Served from 12 to 8 P. M.

(over)

MILLY'S PENSION AND HOME DINING

Wakefield, Massachusetts
Circa 1940

Pensions, although not common in this country, are prevalent in Europe. This one became a popular local restaurant in Massachusetts. Milly is shown bedecked in her native costume in the upper right hand corner.

MOUNT ROYAL HOTEL

Montreal, Canada
Breakfast
Circa 1940

Fish is the major food item listed and some offerings include: Codfish Balls, Fried Haddock, Kippered Herring and Steamed or Creamed Finnan Haddie.

BANFF SPRINGS HOTEL

Banff, Alberta, Canada
August, 1939

This summer resort in the Canadian Rockies was famed for its myriad of summer activities, and nicknamed "Banff the Magnificent." The season began June 15 and ran until September 10. The Banff Springs Hotel was part of the Canadian Pacific hotel chain. (*Opposite*).

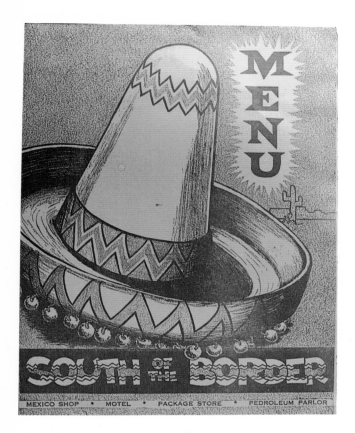

PEDRO'S MAGNIFICENT MOTEL OF TOMORROW

Dillon, South Carolina
1959

The restaurant, called "South of the Border," included a package store, Mexico shop and *Pedroleum* shop. The menu is full of Pedro's little jokes, for example: "f.o.b (full of bull)," "you have to hand it to Pedro—he has a short arm," "Virginia Ham Steak—this ham would tempt a Rabbi!"

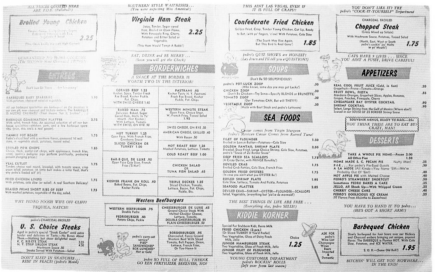

C.L. PERKINS—CONFECTIONER

Boston, Massachusetts
1885

These attractive floral cards were the bill of fare format for this early luncheon and confection shop where soups, sandwiches, salads and desserts were served.

Rathskeller
Under American House, Boston

LADIES AND GENTS DINING ROOM

Boston, Massachusetts
Circa 1900

This is an interesting little menu as it uses a slightly different marketing technique for the period. They pre-sold discount tickets for meals. You received "$1.15 worth for $1.00" if you bought in advance. They advertised "choice *segars* constantly on hand" and claimed to serve the largest sandwiches in Boston. (*Opposite*).

J.N. LANDERS' COFFEE ROOMS

Boston, Massachusetts
June 1, 1904

This was the type of place where a person who was living in a period rooming house might take their meals; the most expensive item is a 65 cent Porter House Steak. There was a special ladies dining room which was open 11 to 2 and 5 to 7:30. Pastry was made on the premises and they were "famed" for their baked beans. On Wednesday and Friday mornings a special of pickled fish and cream with baked potato was served.

THE RATHSKELLER

Boston, Massachusetts
Luncheon
January 5, 1900

This restaurant was attached to the new American House Hotel, and offered a wide variety of German and Hungarian specials along with an extensive general menu.

J. N. LANDERS' COFFEE ROOMS

COR COL-UMBUS AVE AND BERKE-LEY ST   695 WASH-INGTON STREET

OPEN DAY AND NIGHT

LADIES' & GENT'S
DINING ROOM,
JOSEPH F. TURNER,
207 Kneeland Street,
3 Doors East of O.C. Depot.

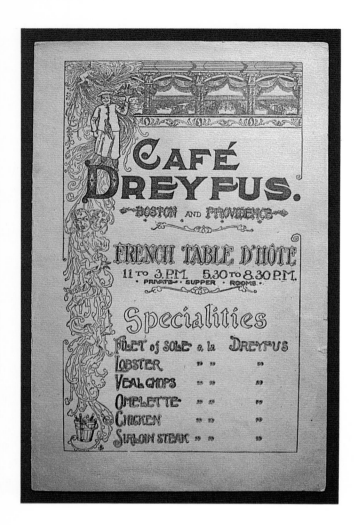

CAFE DREYFUS

Boston, Massachusetts and Providence, Rhode Island
Lunch
October 7, 1904

This plush restaurant offered private supper rooms for intimate parties. A French table d'hote lunch for 35 cents included bisque of lobster, filet of sole au gratin, epigram of lamb, villeroy, pomme nature, lettuce with French dressing, ice cream and cakes or assorted cheese and crackers, and cafe noir. A pint of red wine cost an additional 50 cents.

HEALTH FOOD AND VEGETARIAN DINING ROOM

Boston, Massachusetts
Circa 1900

This claims to be a vegetarian restaurant, but the first three choices on the menu are boiled dinner, breast of lamb, and fried chicken. Each of these entrees is proceeded by the term "VEG."

CAPITAL RESTAURANT

Washington State
Sunday Dinner
1906

This menu is written in what seems to be an Indian dialect, called Chinook Wawa-Wawa. Each course contains highlighted specials: soup—Lukutchee or Spoon Much-A-Muck; boiled—Moos Moos Yaka Tum Tum or Moos Moos Yaka Wawa Wawa; entrees—Siwash Lapool Copopire; vegetables—Waooatoo or Ulalach; desserts—Pil Olally Pie, Totoosh Pie and Kloshe Kahkwa Iktahs.

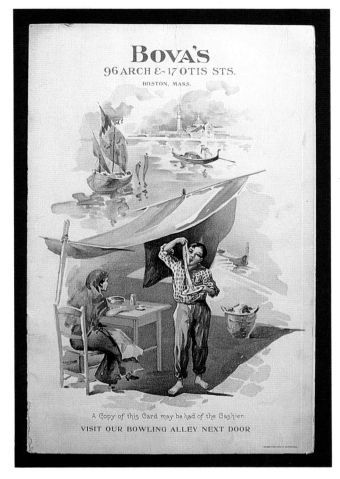

CAFE BOVA

Boston, Massachusetts
Circa 1906

This menu represents a truly ethnic, period Italian restaurant, every menu category written in Italian. Food was served at any time of the day, and a 75 cent ten course dinner including wine and music was served from 5:30 to 7:30 PM, and came with spaghetti, macaroni or noodles cooked to order. The liquor and wine menu was three pages long and mixed drinks, brandies and liquors were sold 15 cents a piece or two for 25 cents. There was also a full page of cigars and cigarettes to choose from. After dining you were invited to visit the owner's bowling alley next door.

ODEON CAFE
San Francisco, California
1908

BISMARCK CAFE AND CATERING CO.

San Francisco, California
1908

Each of these menus was created, designed and printed by Louis Roesch Company of San Francisco. They are not only the menu and wine list for each establishment, but works of art, filled with page after page of unique characterizations depicting the individual establishment. Included are advertisements from vendors graphically designed for each owner's special restaurant. (*Opposite*).

HEIDELBERG INN
San Francisco, California
1908

Menu

HALL'S CENTERPORT L.I.

OLIVES CLAM CHOWDER RADISHES

STEAMED CLAMS-BROTH

FISH IN SEASON

COLD BOILED

SPRING BROILERS MIXED SALAD

STEAMED CORN SHELTER ISLAND

MELON & CREAM

CHEESE COFFEE

ULMER CABINET

SMOKES IMPORTED

ALL BRANDS CIGARETTES MUENCHNER

RIGHT-O

HERE'S TO HALL'S

COPYRIGHT APPLIED FOR

HALL'S FAMOUS SHORE DINNER

$3.00 PER COVER

JOHN WANAMAKER, 1939 NEW YORK WORLD'S FAIR MENU

New York, New York
October 13, 1939

Many special events and programs were planned at this famous department store. (*Top, middle*).

HALL'S FAMOUS SHORE DINNER

Centerport, Long Island
August 18, 1920

"Here's to Hall's" is the toast, echoed by the sun at this stylish shore dinner house. This menu is actually a tri-fold post card mailer. One fold features a map of Long Island indicating that all major roads on Long Island lead to Hall's. The total price for dinner was $3.00. (*Opposite*).

YMCA, 1939 NEW YORK WORLD'S FAIR

New York, New York
1939

"Good rooms, good cheer and a friendly Christian atmosphere" was the motto shown on the back cover with an illustration of twelve resident buildings. (*Bottom, left*).

TURF TRYLON RESTAURANT, 1939 NEW YORK WORLD'S FAIR

New York, New York
1939

The 1939 World's Fair spawned many unique restaurants and concepts. The three menus pictured each mention the theme perisphere. (*Bottom, right*).

PIG 'N WHISTLE

San Francisco, California
August 20, 1939

This souvenir menu has over 20 pages and is intended primarily for children. The interior shows a picture of a magical city along with the story of the Pig 'n Whistle.

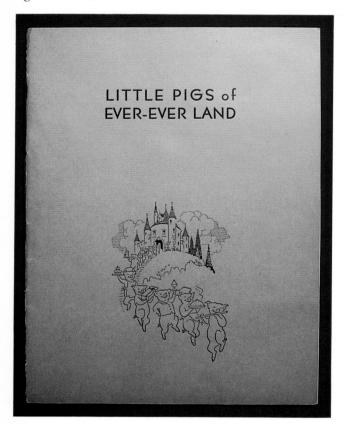

MIKE LYMAN'S GRILL

Los Angeles, California
August 23, 1939

A special note on the menu states: "Our prices on imported and domestic champagnes and wines have been reduced to pre-prohibition levels." Does that mean they served alcohol during prohibition? A "Deluxe Dinner" lists for one dollar, with seven courses in all. Their motto was "the home of steak lovers only."

JACK DEMPSEY'S BROADWAY BAR & COCKTAIL LOUNGE

New York, New York
Luncheon
August 18, 1941

The top of this menu says it all: "The customer is always right," signed below by Jack Dempsey. The menu listed that band leader Irv Carroll was introducing a new instrument called the "Solovox" with Kelly Rand as their singing star.

ANTOINE'S RESTAURANT

Centennial Menu
New Orleans, Louisiana
1940

Founded in 1840 and still operating today, this classic restaurant celebrated its one hundredth birthday in 1940. Beside the menu is a centennial souvenir book full of history, praise and quotes about Antoine's; this is where Oysters Rockefeller was created.

THE TOLL HOUSE

Whitman, Massachusetts
Circa 1940s

This famous restaurant of cookbook fame is no longer with us, but its legacy of the toll house cookie will live on forever. Also shown is a dessert menu and two promotion cards.

HENRICI'S ON RANDOLPH

Chicago, Illinois
Dinner
May 2, 1943

This restaurant was established in 1868, three years after the close of the Civil War and three years before the great Chicago fire. This information and much more American history abounds within. A note in a prominent position announces "No Orchestral Din," loosely translated means "no singing."

WALDORF-ASTORIA

New York, New York
Dinner
October, 1943

This was a special event for the annual N.W.D.A. Dinner. The star-laden event featured Marty May as the Master of Ceremonies, Alfred Drake, Joan Roberts, Celeste Holm, the original cast of "Oklahoma," and dozens of other local and national celebrities.

HOME OF THE GREEN APPLE PIE

Seattle, Washington
1946

This restaurant specialized in salmon, seafood, steaks and apple pie, with Washington State apples as the major pie item. The menu states the one millionth pie was baked on August 24, 1937 and in 1946 they were "well on their way" to the two millionth.

THE GLASS KITCHEN

Lancaster, Pennsylvania
Circa 1948

This restaurant had three different locations and boasts they serve only "scrumptious food." A demonic chef adorns the cover; do not send anything back to the kitchen. Note his cleaver.

BERNSTEIN'S FISH GROTTO

Los Angeles, California
1948

This restaurant offered complete luncheons daily at only 50 cents. They advertised as a fact that fish caught at 5:00 AM was served the same day. One of the captain's dinners was "choppino" or bouillabaisse, an epicurean delight of clams, lobsters, crab, bass, halibut and salmon served in a giant abalone shell for only 90 cents.

SAILOR TOM'S

Reading, Massachusetts
1949

This restaurant offered an adventure as well as a meal; they had a small petting zoo, and part of the restaurant was a large, land-locked ship. They were known for their "Port Hole Specials," and were the home of the "Sea Burger."

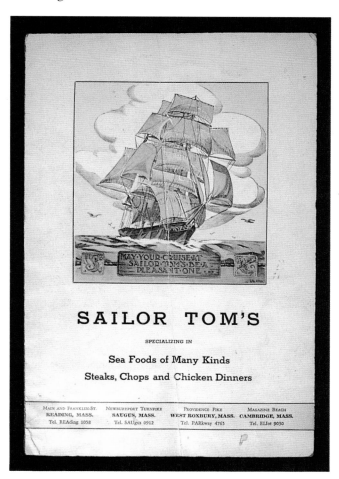

THE GOLDEN PAGODA

Los Angeles, California
1950

This restaurant, other than having a captivating menu cover, offers an interesting dining plan of differently priced dinners: 85 cents per person, $1.15 per person and the Chinese Dinner Deluxe for $1.50 per person. A greater variety of dishes was available when more people were served.

VALLE'S STEAK HOUSE

Portland, Maine
Circa 1950s

This restaurant, founded in 1933, stayed in this location until 1960. They expanded and created a major chain of properties on the East Coast. They were known for steaks, twin lobster specials and large portions at reasonable prices. A postcard mailer is also shown and states the restaurant is a mecca for tourists and traveling men.

Steaks fit for a King...

THE RUSSIAN TEA ROOM

New York, New York
Circa 1950s

This menu cover is actually an artist's proof for final design approval; the color and design is truly unique. The Russian Tea Room still exists in New York. (*Opposite*).

The Russian Tea Room

AL SCHACHT'S SCORE CARD

WHEN IT COMES
TO FOOD —
I'M NOT
CLOWNING

I'M HERE

MENU USED AT CIRCUS SAINTS & SINNERS LUNCHEON
(Waldorf-Astoria) HONORING AL SCHACHT as FALL GUY

S C O R E   C A R D

Al Schacht's **RESTAURANT**
Where the Screw Balls Meat
102 East 52nd St., New York City
DEMOCRATIC WAITERS—REPUBLICAN PRICES

May We Exchange Autographs ????

1. Yours..................................
2. Address............printed!!!!!
   City..................................
3. Birthday..................................
   month   day
   (The secret of the year stays with you)
4. Anniversary..................................
   (or what have you)   month   day

Cordially

AL SCHACHT'S SCORE CARD RESTAURANT

New York, New York
1950.

This was a real meeting place for baseball enthusiasts; each menu was signed by the owner if requested. The back cover displayed the all-time, all-star team as voted by the customers and includes the following quote: "We know it's tough to pay $4.75 for a steak, but if you want something really tough, try our $2.00 steak."

HOWARD JOHNSON'S RESTAURANTS

The New England Area
1940s and 1950s

Known as "the landmark for hungry Americans," these orange roofed restaurants stretched from Maine to New York. Their trademark was Simple Simon and the Pie Man, and their early slogan was "Like Simple Simon we all must eat—and Howard Johnson's can't be beat!" They also invented the clam strip dinner.

HARROW'S RUSTIC ROOST

Reading, Massachusetts

Circa 1955

This restaurant still exists, but is now called Harrow's. The menu is basically the same, but the prices are a little higher. They still do their own baking and serve great fried chicken and chicken pie dinners.

PSCHORR-BRAU

Ausfchank, Berlin, Germany

Lunch

September 23, 1898

This represents the Pschorr-Brewery's tavern menu, or mid-morning meal list or card. The bottom portion of the cover details delivery information and costs for bottled beer and beer shipped in barrels.

RISTORANTE ULPIA

Rome, Italy
April 4, 1928

The same restaurant reflecting a new style of menu five years later.

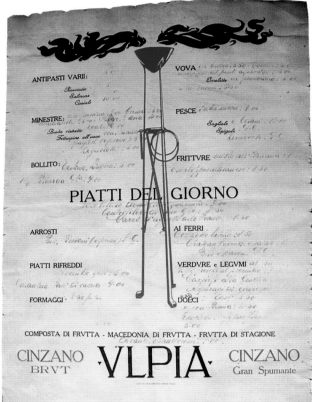

RISTORANTE ULPIA

Rome, Italy
March 20, 1923

A very original and aristocratic menu by virtue of the prices and items offered, this restaurant was located in an excellent and ancient area of Rome. Also shown is a postcard and a private wine label of the restaurant.

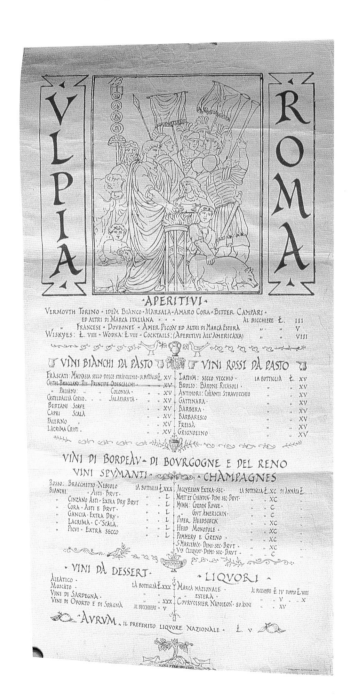

RESTAURANT DU BOEUF A LA MODE

Paris, France
April, 1923

This restaurant, founded in 1792, was noted for its small private rooms and fine cuisine. The adorned steer represents the insignia of the restaurant and symbolically relates to adorning the menu's beef dishes.

SAVOY RESTAURANT

London, England
April 4, 1923

The menus shown represent a private luncheon shared by a group of friends on a European tour. They are beautifully designed with a period motif.

"ROMANO"

PARIS   14, RUE CAUMARTIN

DyL

CARTE DE LA SOIREE

— AYALA —	— HEIDSIECK & Cⁱᵉ —	— POMMERY & GRENO —
200 Goût Américain (Cuvée Sᵗᵉ	229 Monopole dry........50	251 Drapeau américain......50
201 Brut) Romano 45	230 Monopole 1911.......55	252 Nature..............50
202 Brut 1915 50	— HEIDSIECK Charles —	— PIPER HEIDSIECK —
— CORDON ROUGE —	231 Goût Américain......50	253 Brut 1914............50
210 Cordon rouge.........60	232 Brut England 1911..55	254 Brut 1911............55
211 Cordon rouge 1911....65	233 Brut 1906...........60	— POL ROGER —
212 Cordon rouge 1906....70	— IRROY —	256 Brut 1914............50
— Vᵛᵉ CLICQUOT PONSARDIN —	234 Goût américain......50	257 Brut 1911............50
213 Carte jaune extra dry 55	235 Brut 1911...........55	258 Brut 1906............65
214 Brut 1911............60	— KRUG —	— ROEDERER —
215 Brut 1906............70	236 Extra sec...........50	260 Extra sec...........50
— DELBECK HELIOS —	238 Brut 1911...........55	261 Brut 1911...........55
216 Brut 1911............50	239 Brut 1906...........60	— RUINART —
216bis Delbeck demi-sec...50	— LANSON —	262 La Maréchal demi-sec...50
— DUMINY —	240 Brut réserve........50	263 Brut 1911...........55
220 Carte d'Or..........50	242 Brut 1911...........60	264 Carte anglaise 1906...60
221 Brut cape rouge......50	243 Brut 1906...........65	— KENEL DUBAIL —
222 Brut 1915...........55	— MOET & CHANDON —	267 Brut 1915...........55
— GEORGE GOULET —	244 Brut Impérial 1911..60	268 Brut................50
224 Goût américain.......50	245 Brut Impérial 1906..65	— LEMAITRE —
226 Brut 1914...........55	246 Brut Impérial 1904..70	269 Lemaître 1915.........50

Consommations diverses prix unique........6   Whisky............10

Après 10 heures le champagne ou la consommation est obligatoire.
Taxe Assistance & Etat....25 %

Il est offert gracieusement une assiette de petits fours par bouteille de
Champagne — L'assiette supplémentaire...........3 frs.

Imp. Robillon: 17,R. du Terrage-Paris

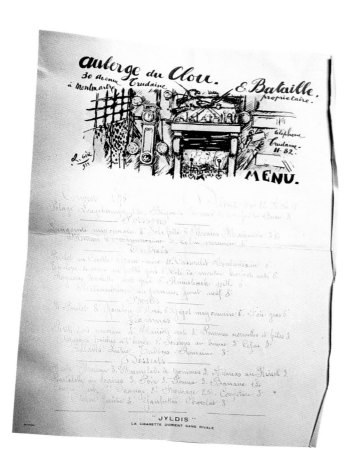

AUBERGE DU CLOU

Montmartre, France
April 11, 1923

The restaurant, steeped in tradition and extremely picturesque, was founded in 1883, and offered a unique formal dining experience. Shown also are postcards and a business card.

ROMANO RESTAURANT

Paris, France
April 1923

This is a wine and champagne list; Romano appears to be a restaurant with entertainment, after 6 PM consumption of alcoholic beverages was required. Complimentary petit fours were presented with each bottle of champagne.

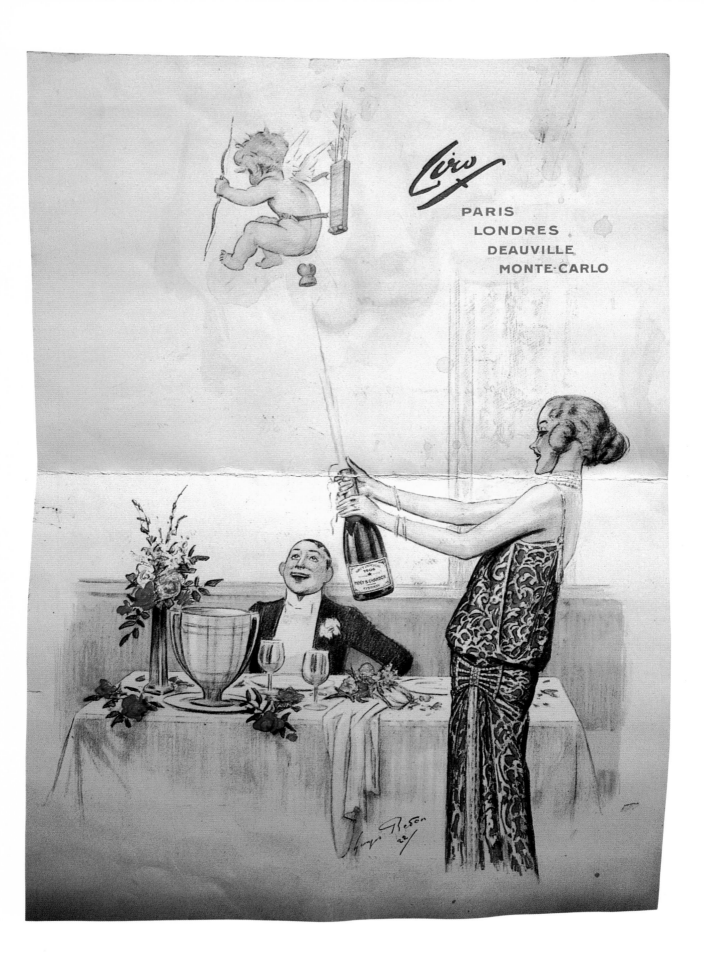

TRICITY RESTAURANT

At the top of Savoy Hill in the Strand
London, England
March, 1927

These specially shaped mini-menus describe the state-of-the art electric cooking and lighting effects in the restaurant. The cocktail shaker-shaped menu is a wine and cocktail list.

CIRO

Paris, France
April 12, 1923

Ciro's had sister restaurants in London, Deauville and Monte Carlo. This classic period restaurant is a perfect representation of the carefree life appreciated by the very rich. The listed cover charge is extremely high for such an early date.

D'AGORNO

Paris, France
Circa 1920s

D'Agorno's menu states they offer the best grilled items, reasonably priced. The restaurant's credo was "all menu items are cooked at ease to the wishes of our customers," but with the caveat, "know how to order and you will be well-served."

EDOUARD ROUZIER, ROTISSERIE PERIGOURDINE

Paris, France
1927

"The temple of the gourmets," this restaurant specialized in rotisserie items and encouraged small and large private parties. The rather humorous design features geese holding a banner, and a man and a pig, called "the collaborateurs," rooting out truffles for the table.

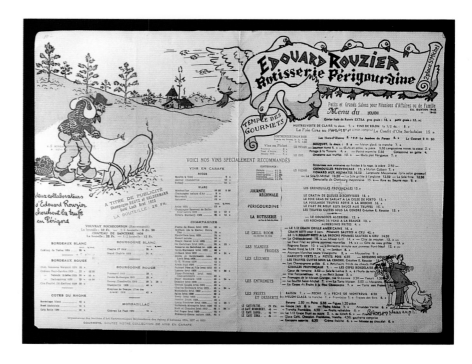

KAKUK RESTAURANT

Budapest, Hungary
Circa 1936

This period restaurant menu contains choices written in Hungarian and French. Inside, the word "Etlap" appears which means menu or list. A champagne ad for a brand called "Littke" is printed in the corner.

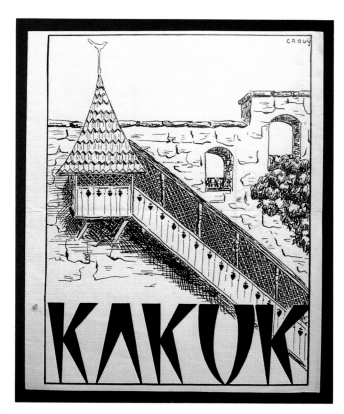

MAISON PRUNIER

Paris, France
April and July, 1936

This restaurant advertises they serve everything coming from the sea. A sister restaurant existed in London and was also moderately priced with no cover charge. Each month, the cover design changed.

AXAIA (ACHAIA)

Athens, Greece
October 17, 1952

This tourist restaurant in Greece utilized a menu written in English and French. Some Greek headings were listed with pictures of beer to entice the clientele.

RISTORANTE SABATINI

Florence, Italy
1952

This booklet represents a tourist's menu, common in large, European cities. No prices are listed, as they often changed depending upon who was eating there and the mood of the server.

CAFE DE LA PAIX

Paris, France
October 12, 1955

Located near the opera house in Paris, this cafe is very popular, and offers a wide variety of specials for all hours of the day. A weekly calendar of special meals and an extensive champagne and wine list are other features of this bill of fare. (*Opposite*).

7 SMAA HJEM (SEVEN LITTLE HOMES) RESTAURANT

Copenhagen, Denmark
1960

This menu, actually a multi-fold postcard mailer, features all the menu items at the restaurant, as well as detailing many points of interest in Copenhagen, including the famous Tivoli Gardens.

Reception and Banquet

Col. Charles A. Lindbergh

BANQUET HALL
BEKTASH TEMPLE

CONCORD, N. H.
JULY 25, 1927

3

Celebrate

MENUS FROM
SPECIAL EVENTS

*T*he old adage, "We are judged by the company we keep" means a great deal in this menu category. It is human nature to want to be seen as a part of a special group, and to take members of those groups and elevate them to positions of honor. It does not matter if the group is political, work related or fraternal; human nature desires to honor leaders in every aspect of life, and a luncheon or dinner is a way to celebrate and distinguish these chosen few.

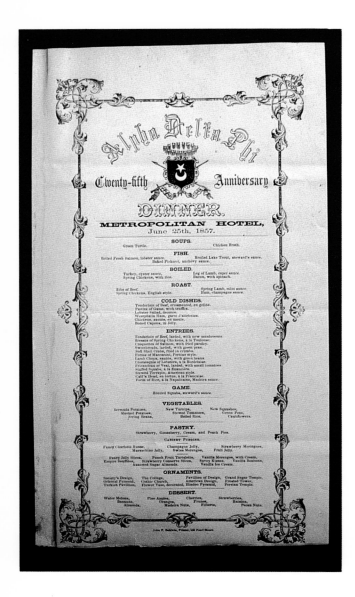

ALPHA DELTA PHI—TWENTY-FIFTH ANNIVERSARY DINNER

Metropolitan Hotel, New York, New York
June 25, 1857

This menu, printed on a heavy paper stock, is in a bill of fare format. Eleven courses are offered, with the ornamental course representing a creative presentation designed in a food media that included pieces depicting the fraternal society and the college.

ANNUAL SUPPER OF THE MASTER MARINERS ASSOCIATION

Morgan's Academy Hall (State Unknown)
Location Unknown
December 9, 1890

This hand painted side fold menu is quite small, with the cover scene depicting a coastal schooner running before the wind. The back side of the jacket lists the officers and committee members of the Association, along with a picture of a buoy.

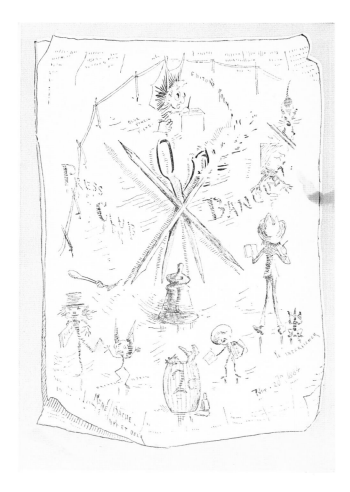

THE COAL CLUB OF BOSTON AND VICINITY DINNER

Young's Hotel
Boston, Massachusetts
January 26, 1893

This bill of fare style menu represents a pre-designed card that allowed the printer or hotel to add the menu as needed. There is one very unusual dessert listed: The Rum Fromage.

PRESS CLUB BANQUET

Delmonico's
New York, New York
November 20, 1884

The cover of this menu is a pen and ink drawing featuring the functions of a reporter in parody; careful scrutiny reveals little ink gremlins and hidden messages. Each course is accented by humorous puns. The toasts are entitled "The Oratorical Feast." The back cover lists all of the Press Club's officers.

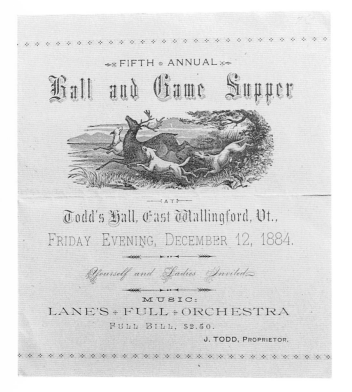

FIFTH ANNUAL BALL AND GAME SUPPER

Todd's Hall
East Wallingford, Connecticut
December 12, 1884

This special menu represents a dinner style that cannot be recreated today. It offers four varieties of duck, black bear, wild turkey, saddle of venison and assorted game birds. The cover pictures a stag being brought down by a pack of hunting dogs. The invitation is addressed to "Yourself and Ladies," with the full bill for the meal listed at $2.50.

THE NEW HAMPSHIRE CLUB, LADIES DAY

The Revere House
Boston, Massachusetts
February 9, 1887

This heavy cardboard menu with beveled, gilded edges, features a pinecone laden bough accenting a painted scene of a canoeist. The covers are secured at the top with a large, white satin ribbon. This pre-designed folder was created by John A. Lowell & Company, Boston. (*Opposite*).

John A Lowell & Co Boston. 532

LE PRE CATELAN DINNER

Location Unknown
1890

This lightweight, cardboard menu is hand designed and painted with the signature of the artist. The interior menu, written in French, is quite faded and barely legible. The back is signed by many of the attendees.

THE SECOND ANNUAL MEETING AND DINNER OF THE COMMODORE CLUB

The Parker House
Boston, Massachusetts
February 1, 1890

This hand designed menu front features a hanging game bird with the club name written in gold ink. The heavy parchment is secured to the cabinet with two pink ribbons. The menu is written in a satirical manner with humorous entrees in each course: white birch soup, boiled ram, roast crow, fried muskrat, stewed eagles, caribou liver a'la McGinty; the beverages were listed as "lubricators." The menu begins with the verse "and the band played Annie Laurie."

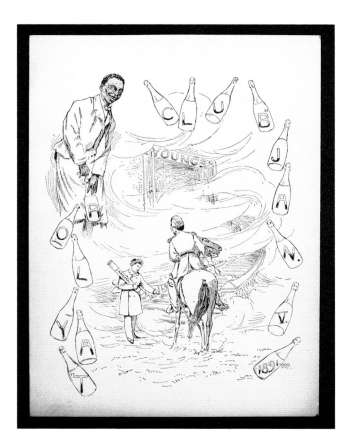

INAUGURAL DINNER OF THE TAYLOR CLUB

Young's Hotel
Boston, Massachusetts
January 5, 1891

This pen-and-ink design menu represents a tongue-in-cheek review of the club's history and honored the mayor-elect of Cambridge, Massachusetts, the Honorable A.B. Alger. The bill of fare includes reference to the circulation of the Boston Globe and a number of regional events. Each course is accented with humorous or old verse.

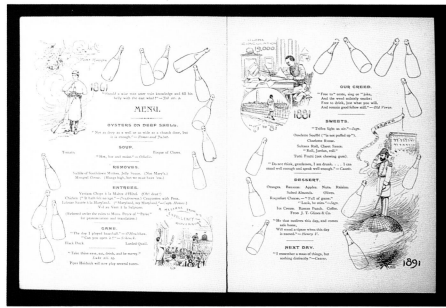

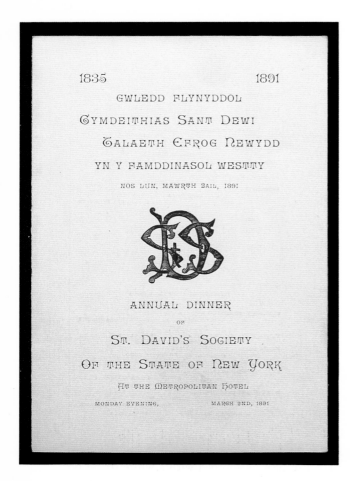

1835   1891

GWLEDD FLYNYDDOL

GYMDEITHIAS SANT DEWI

TALAETH EFROG NEWYDD

YN Y FAMDDINASOL WESTTY

NOS LUN, MAWRTH 2AIL, 1891

ANNUAL DINNER

OF

ST. DAVID'S SOCIETY

OF THE STATE OF NEW YORK

AT THE METROPOLITAN HOTEL

MONDAY EVENING,   MARCH 2ND, 1891

ANNUAL DINNER OF THE SAINT DAVID'S SOCIETY OF THE STATE OF NEW YORK

The Metropolitan Hotel,
New York, New York
March 2, 1891

This light green menu does not have the drama of some, but the intertwined red letters of the society's name form their unique logo. Written partially in Welsh, the messages that accompany each toast are quite impressive, such as "Woman—she honors us tonight by her presence. May we never forget that she is our companion, our friend, and our equal in all things in which she is not our superior."

DINNER TO THE DIRECTORS OF THE BERKSHIRE COTTON MFG. COMPANY

Location Unknown
July 30, 1891

The cover pictures a bronze lobster and a silver crab climbing a golden menu. At the bottom is printed the name of one of the attendees. The menu selections are a wonderful example of a summer shore dinner: Little Neck clams, fish and clam chowder, clam fritters, broiled bluefish, baked clams, baked lobster, baked sweet potatoes and corn, dressed lobster, Boston brown bread, and for dessert, Kitemaug pudding.

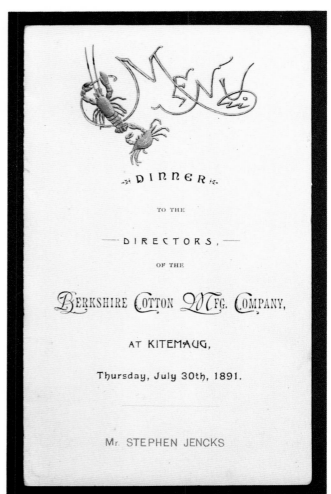

MENU

DINNER

TO THE

DIRECTORS,

OF THE

BERKSHIRE COTTON MFG. COMPANY,

AT KITEMAUG,

Thursday, July 30th, 1891.

Mr. STEPHEN JENCKS

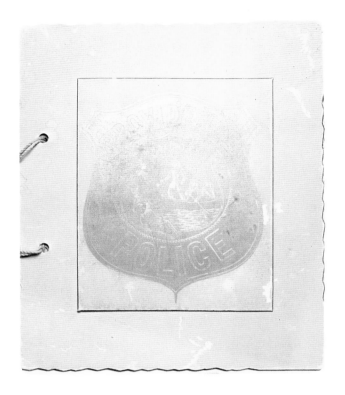

TENTH ANNUAL CONCERT AND BALL OF THE PROVIDENCE POLICE ASSOCIATION

Infantry Hall
Providence, Rhode Island
December 8, 1892

This cardboard cabinet bares a silver-inked badge on the cover which reads in capital letters: "PROVIDENCE POLICE," and in small letters above a pilgrim scene, "what cheer." Along with supper, dancing and toasts, there was a mini-play entitled "Episodes of a Policeman's Life." The price for tickets was 75 cents, including supper. On the back of the menu is an engraving of a policeman in period uniform.

NEW HAMPSHIRE CLUB LADIES DAY

Revere House
Boston, Massachusetts
February 15, 1893

This menu features a cover of embossed white board, fastened to the jacket with four small brass rivets. The organization's name, written in gold ink on a laminated surface, is adorned with a white string bow.

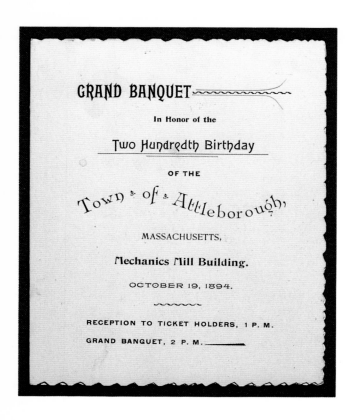

GRAND BANQUET IN HONOR OF THE TWO HUNDREDTH BIRTHDAY OF THE TOWN OF ATTLEBOROUGH

Mechanics Mill Building
Attleborough, Massachusetts
October 19, 1894

The cover of this menu is quite simple, but the item of interest is the speaker's agenda, headed with the term "Post-Prandial" (which means: after the meal). This term is not usually associated with menus since most of the speakers were politicians, noted for their "long-windedness." At the end of the toast and speaker's list is the statement, "If time permits, other speakers may be expected"; a subtle way of asking for short speeches.

RECEPTION AND DINNER TENDERED TO J. FRANCIS HAYWARD

United States Hotel
Boston, Massachusetts
April 2, 1897

This event, sponsored by Mr. Hayward's employees, was held on the occasion of his return from Europe. There were four branch stores involved: the Lowell Rubber Company, Lowell, Massachusetts; the Hope Rubber Company, Providence, Rhode Island; The Lawrence Rubber Company, Lawrence, Massachusetts; and the Fall River Rubber Company, Fall River, Massachusetts. It seems his employees gave him frequent dinners as a number of other menus from the same year exist, honoring him for no apparent reason or occasion.

PENTAGON CLUB DINNER

United States Hotel
Boston, Massachusetts
April 24, 1897

This pre-designed menu cabinet shows a winter scene with a bouquet of spring flowers, to signify the changing of seasons. The menu choices are simple, but one item of interest offered was freshly caught bluefish. (*Opposite*).

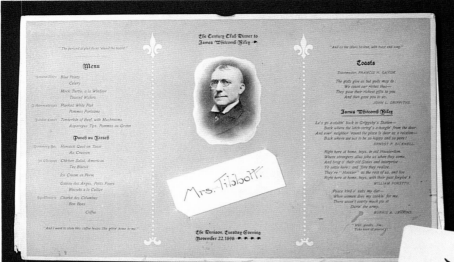

DINNER TO JAMES WHITCOMB RILEY

The Denison
Indianapolis, Indiana
November 22, 1898

This special welcome menu displays a close relation-
ship between the event hosts and James Whitcomb
Riley, as expressed by the special quotes throughout.
The design is rather interesting; the menu is comprised
of two sections with the rear section folding to form an
easel to support the menu card itself. Two small cuts in
the front are used to accommodate a small name card,
indicating that the menu doubled as a place card.

FIRST ANNUAL DINNER OF
THE LAURENTIAN CLUB

Holland House
New York, New York
March 10, 1899

The term "Laurentian" refers to the St. Lawrence
River. This menu cover would seem to depict the
meeting of a Canadian and American club, that might
have a conservationist or naturalist direction. The
crossed flags with a small wreath of holly accent the
natural canoeing scene. The menu itself is written
totally in French.

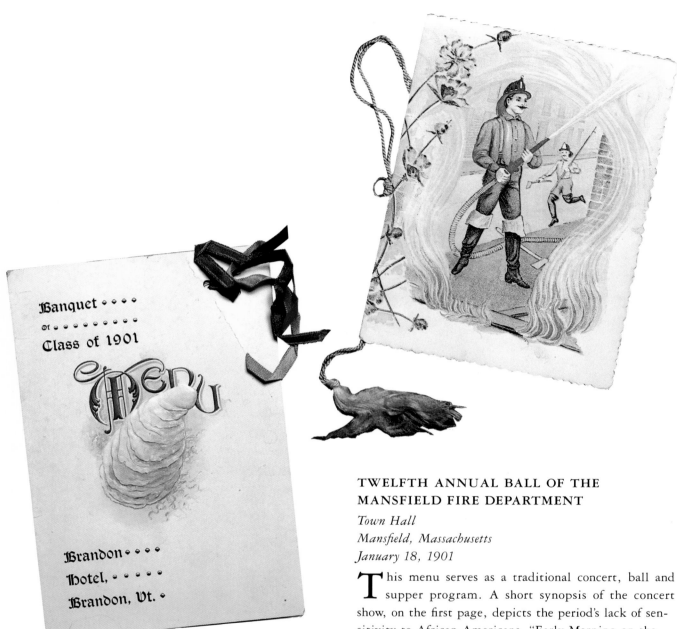

BANQUET OF THE CLASS OF 1901

Brandon Hotel
Brandon, Vermont
1901

This may have been a graduation dinner, as there is much discussion of things to come and plans to be made. The toasts on the back of the menu jacket offer superb grist for any mill, for example: "A man not of words, but of action, offers his hand and his heart."

TWELFTH ANNUAL BALL OF THE MANSFIELD FIRE DEPARTMENT

Town Hall
Mansfield, Massachusetts
January 18, 1901

This menu serves as a traditional concert, ball and supper program. A short synopsis of the concert show, on the first page, depicts the period's lack of sensitivity to African Americans. "Early Morning on the river—steamboats passing—plantation bell ringing—darkies singing—caliope playing—boat approaching the landing to wood up—chorus of the darkies as they load up the wood—'All Aboard'—boat starts down the river—niggers on deck enjoying themselves by singing, etc. 'Hurrah! Hurrah! Here comes the race!'—which ends in an explosion."

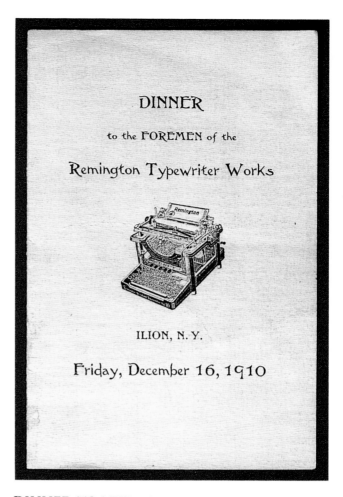

BLUE HILL STREET RAILWAY EMPLOYEES, MUTUAL AID ASSOCIATION SECOND GRAND CONCERT AND BALL

Memorial Hall
Canton, Massachusetts
January 29, 1904

The cover features a picture of an electric trolley car which ran on the Blue Hill Street line. It was very common to combine a concert ball and supper, to promote company loyalty.

DINNER TO THE FOREMEN OF THE REMINGTON TYPEWRITER WORKS

Ilion, New York
December 16, 1910

This little menu cover pictures an early model of a Remington Typewriter. The interior outlines the musical program and the menu, including a musical descriptive entitled "A Hunt in the Black Forest."

ANNUAL BANQUET AND REUNION OF THE MASSACHUSETTS PRESS ASSOCIATION

United States Hotel
Boston Massachusetts
January 14, 1907

This menu cover features embossed carnations beside a portrait of a pond and countryside. The jacket is decorated with a paper topped frilled toothpick and a red velvet bow. The featured speakers were the Lieutenant Governor of Massachusetts and the Mayor of Boston. All of the attendees were invited after dinner to witness the productions at the Hollis Theater and Majestic Theater as the guests of the management.

ANNIVERSARY BANQUET FOR THE FORESTERS OF AMERICA

C.C. Whittlemore Caterer
Boston, Massachusetts
January 7, 1912

This fraternal order was part of the court pioneer number 137 of the Foresters of America. Their credo was "Liberty, Unity Benevolence and Concord." The menu cover represents their seal and logo. The events of the evening included dinner, the annual meeting, music and a humorist named A. Papineau.

FOURTEENTH ANNIVERSARY ESWOD

Location Unknown
February 29, 1912

This artist's proof for a menu cover seems as if it was designed for a men's stag dinner or a smoker.

DINNER TO THE AMERICAN ELECTRIC RAILWAY ASSOCIATION — GIVEN BY THE AMERICAN ELECTRIC RAILWAY MANUFACTURERS ASSOCIATION

Hotel Astor
New York, New York
January 31, 1913

The cover of this menu is highly interesting as it depicts the history of the electric trolley car. The three flags represent the United States, Canada and Mexico, while the gold and blue seal represent the initials of the association, with their seal on the back side. The menu is bound with a silver-colored cord.

MENU

Shore Dinner

For Ladies

COLEBROOK HOUSE,
COLEBROOK, N. H.

N. B. LADD.

WEDNESDAY EVENING, FEBRUARY 5, 1913.

SHORE DINNER FOR THE LADIES

Colebrook House
Colebrook, New Hampshire
February 5, 1913

This interesting menu features a toast-mistress, which was highly unusual for the period. The fanciful cover design includes a mermaid, dolphins and chubby little sea cherubs. The fare was a traditional New Hampshire shore dinner with one surprising course, Rhode Island steamers.

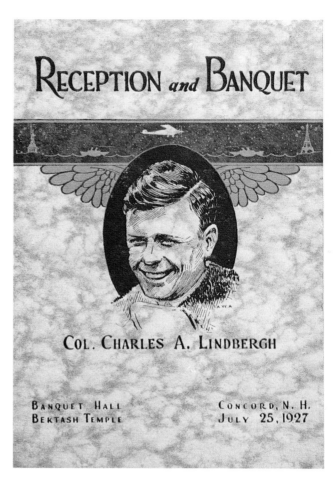

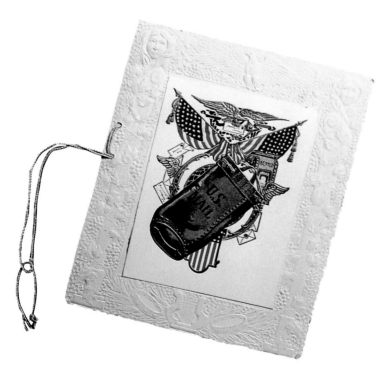

TWENTY-THIRD ANNUAL MASSACHUSETTS STATE CONVENTION OF LETTER CARRIERS

O. P. Sullivan Caterers
Salem, Massachusetts
May 2, 1915

This embossed white menu features a centered assembly of postal tribute which includes flags, eagles, letters, a mailbox and an early mail bag. The back page of the menu features a poem by Grace Courtland, "The Faithful Postman."

RECEPTION AND BANQUET FOR COLONEL CHARLES A. LINDBERGH

Banquet Hall, Bektash Temple
Concord, New Hampshire
July 25, 1927

This bill of fare is designed to resemble a field of clouds on which floats a portrait of Charles Lindbergh. Above his head is a gold panorama featuring the Statue of Liberty and the Eiffel Tower with the spirit of Saint Louis flying in between to symbolically portray the first trans-Atlantic flight. This was a major event for Concord, New Hampshire, as the governor, the mayor and the state senator were all in attendance. There were also eight other mayors from major New England cities in the reception line.

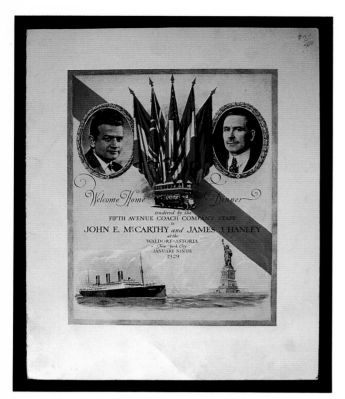

WELCOME HOME DINNER TO JOHN E. McCARTHY AND JAMES J. HANLEY TENDERED BY THE FIFTH AVENUE COACH COMPANY STAFF

The Waldorf Astoria
New York, New York
January 9, 1929

The flags on the front of the menu represent all of the countries the two gentlemen visited. They went abroad to study the manufacturing techniques of European coach builders. The inner cover has a reproduction of the hand written manuscript of the song "America" written in 1832 by S.F. Smith. Inside the menu was a folded song sheet titled "Home Again." Composed for and sung at the welcome home dinner, it had eighteen stanzas with a chorus between each.

TESTIMONIAL BANQUET TENDERED TO FREDERICK E. HAWLEY GREAT SACHEM OF MASSACHUSETTS

Mansion House
Greenfield, Massachusetts
January 9, 1932

This dinner, given by the Connecticut Red Man's Council, is for a fraternal organization. The menu is full of songs sung that evening; they ranged from "America" to "When Your Hair Has Turned to Silver." There were also great door prizes, a $5.00 gold piece from the Picomegan tribe; a flashlight, donated by Leon Whitmore; and numerous others with the last prize being a case of Boynton's Pale Dry Ginger Ale.

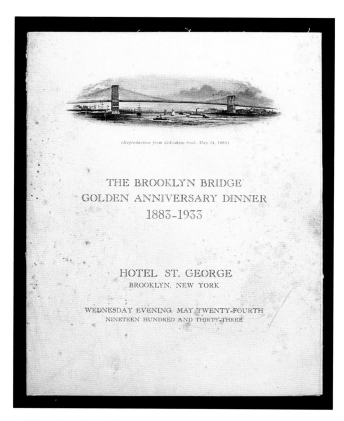

THE BROOKLYN BRIDGE GOLDEN ANNIVERSARY DINNER

Hotel St. George
Brooklyn, New York
May 24, 1933

This is a tri-fold menu, with the cover boasting a reproduction of the picture from the May 24, 1883 bridge dedication book. Each facing page of this menu has a reproduction of the comparable information reproduced from the 1883 dedication book.

WEDDING DINNER FOR JOSEPH AND RUTH GREENSTEIN

Jefferson Manor
Philadelphia, Pennsylvania
November 28, 1937

This menu page is the actual contract for a wedding dinner. The ceremony was held in the Pink Room and the dinner was served in the Crystal Room at the Jefferson Manor. The dinner was paid for by the bride's mother, Mrs. Anna Dunn, at the cost of $1.40 per person, including beer.

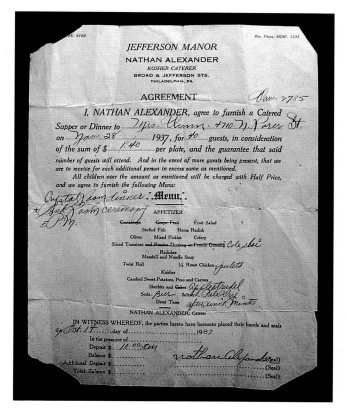

Dinner   in honour of

His Excellency
PAUL W. CLAUDEL
AMBASSADOR OF FRANCE
given by the
ASSUMPTION COLLEGE
OF WORCESTER, MASSACHUSETTS

April fifteen
Nineteen twenty-nine

Bancroft Hotel
Worcester

4

You're A Grand Old Flag

MENUS FROM POLITICAL AND PATRIOTIC EVENTS

*T*he military and political systems have always been a base for social interaction. By their nature, they require meetings, dinners and reunions, as governments must honor dignitaries and heads of state, political and military leaders receive testimonials, heros require banquets and military units need to come together and relive their great moments.

The following menus represent a few of those events.

GRAND CENTENNIAL MILITARY AND CIVIC BALL

Sponsored by The Centennial Committee
Agricultural Hall
Concord, Massachusetts
April 19, 1875

This event commemorated the "shot heard round the world" at the Old North Bridge in Concord, Massachusetts. The menu has four pages with the first inner cover listing all the committee members and their leadership. The musical portion featured three bands: the U.S. Marine Band, Brown & Reeve's Orchestra of Providence and Carter's Orchestra of Boston. This was a very late evening; there was a promenade concert from 8 PM until 10 PM, dancing at 10 PM and supper at 11 PM.

SOCIETY OF THE ARMY OF THE POTOMAC: EIGHTEENTH ANNUAL REUNION AND BANQUET

Sponsored by the Society of the Army of the Potomac
Congress Hall
Saratoga, New York
June 23, 1887

This impressive period dinner was resplendent with ornamental food sculpture depicting various historic scenes and places—the capture of Richmond, Fort Sumpter, The Horn of Plenty, the Burning of Congress, the Army of the Potomac, and the Pyramid of the Grand Republic. The meal included 14 toasts beginning with the President's and ending with the poet of the evening. They drank well; courses included Vino de Pasto, St. Julien wine, G.H. Mumm extra dry champagne and Monongahela monogram whiskey.

NINTH INTERNATIONAL CONGRESS BANQUET

Sponsored by The Committee
Washington, District of Columbia
September, 1887

This menu features four gilded cardboard pages. The front cover has Lady Liberty with the official seals of the original 13 states overhead and the seals of the then existing 26 states at her feet; she symbolically stands on the top of a globe of the world. Each of the pages has a cartoon in the upper lefthand corner. One features Lady Liberty cooking for each of the state's delegates; the second page features Uncle Sam opening bottles of champagne above the official seals of the six great powers. The back page features an American Eagle and the flags of the six great powers wrapped in the protective drape of the United States flag.

COMPLIMENTARY DINNER TO THE HON. P.A. COLLINS, CHAIRMAN OF THE DEMOCRATIC NATIONAL CONVENTION, AND HIS ASSOCIATE DELEGATES TO ST. LOUIS

Sponsored by the Bay State Club
The Revere House
Boston, Massachusetts
June 16, 1888

COMPLIMENTARY DINNER TO THE NOMINEES ON THE DEMOCRATIC STATE TICKET

Sponsored by the Bay State Club
Revere House
Boston, Massachusetts
September 15, 1888

Both of these menu covers were identical, they featured the names of the Democratic Nominees for President and Vice President of the United States, Cleveland and Thurman. The June event had the hard beveled cardboard covers tied at the top with a pink ribbon, while the September event had the covers tied at the side with two red ribbons. The back cover of the June menu featured an American Eagle while the back cover of the September dinner featured engravings of Cleveland and Thurman. The menu choices were practically identical.

ELECTION COMMITTEE DINNER

Sponsored by the Central Club of Boston
The Club House
Boston, Massachusetts
May 23, 1889

The single fold covers of this menu are light cardboard with fluted edges; handpainted yellow flowers adorn the cover. This menu contains the wine listing for every course: soup—Old Cabinet Sherry; fish—Chateau Yquem, 1874; entrees—Chateau Mouton, 1869; removes—Private Club; relieve—Roman Punch; game—Chambertin; dessert—Cognac.

ANNIVERSARY DINNER

Sponsored by the Boston Light
Infantry Veteran Corps
The Fitchburg Hotel
Fitchburg, Massachusetts
October 18, 1889

This light cardboard folder features the Boston Light Infantry Insignia of a stalking tiger with the motto "Aut Morior Aut Honeste Vivere" upon a raised white background. The back of the menu has the insignia of the Fitchburg Hotel.

DINNER TO CAPT. LOUIS PHILIPPE D'ORLEANS, COMTE DE PARIS

Sponsored by the Comrades of the Army of the Potomac
The Plaza Hotel
New York, New York
October 20, 1890

This menu is constructed of three pieces of light cardboard tied at the top with white ribbon. The medal at the top left of the cover is the insignia of the Army of the Potomac. The name at the bottom is in gold ink and represents the officers' seating placement. The menu is in French and offers 10 courses, each with wine and liqueurs with dessert.

FIRST ANNUAL DINNER

Sponsored by the Naval Academy Alumni
Association of New York
Delmonico's
New York, New York
January 23, 1897

The light cardboard menu jacket contains a paper insert. The cover pictures George Bancroft, the founder of the Naval Academy. The menu page is in French, with the "Ode to the Jolly Mariner" at the top. There were 10 toasts including the President's Toast given by Vice President Stevenson and "A Toast to Harvard—Memorial Hall and What It Means," given by Mr. Theodore Roosevelt.

TWENTY-FIRST ANNIVERSARY, THE COMMANDERY OF THE STATE OF CALIFORNIA

Sponsored by the Commandery Committee
Pioneer Hall
San Francisco, California
Tuesday, May 3 and Wednesday, May 4, 1892

This menu, crafted of light cardboard with 11 pages, is tied with a red and blue ribbon at the top. The cover shows a raised, hand-tinted engraving of the commandery medal. Page one has an engraving of soldiers on horseback announcing the anniversary. Page two has an engraving of the bay with ships detailing Ladies Day, May 3rd. Page four has an engraving of a cannon with flowers growing from it and doves flying; this page announces the dinner on May 4th. Page five is the menu with each course described with verse. Page six has an engraving of a canteen with the wine list and a verse for each course; six champagnes were served at this meal. Page seven has an engraving of a battery of cannons firing at the top and the toasts and their text on the next two pages. Page nine lists all the commanders since 1871; page 10 has an engraving of a soldier on watch, entitled "Taps." (*Opposite*).

THE ROYAL LUNCHEON & HER MAJESTY'S DINNER

Sponsored by Queen Victoria's Court
Windsor Castle
Dinner: December 17, 1894
Luncheon: November 23, 1899

Both menus reflect the daily fare at the castle; these do not appear to be special meals of state. The printed menu is in French while the handwritten dinner menu is a combination of English and French.

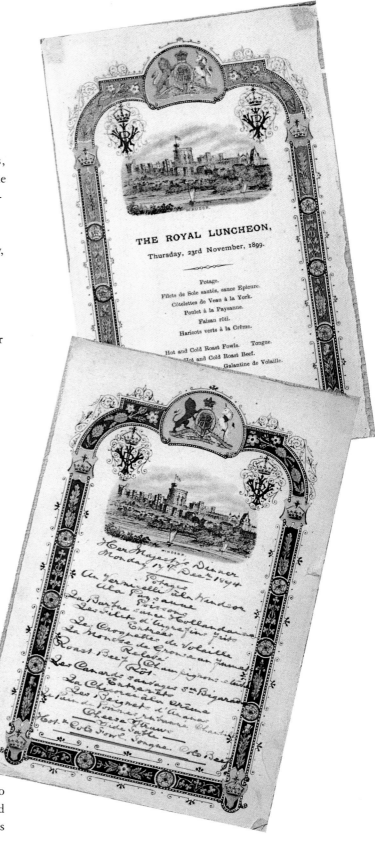

DINNER IN HONOR OF HIS ROYAL
HIGHLIGHTS PRINCE HENRY OF PRUSSIA

Sponsored by the City of Boston
The Hotel Somerset
Boston, Massachusetts
March 6, 1902

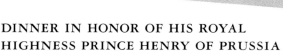

T he cover of this menu is adorned by a gray oval background embossed with crossed flags of the United States and Prussia. The shields of the countries appear on both sides of the royal armor, encircled by a raised, gilded ribbon frame. The menu is bound with a large red, white and blue ribbon with stamped golden eagles. The first page has an engraved portrait of the Prince over the dinner announcement. The menu is in English and features New England fare. The back cover of the menu has a golden, Boston Condita Seal.

FAREWELL DINNER TO
GENERAL HORACE PORTER, AMBASSADOR
FROM THE UNITED STATES TO
THE REPUBLIC OF FRANCE

Sponsored by the New York Commandery of the
Loyal Order of the Loyal Legion of the United States,
by his companions of the Order
Delmonico's
New York, New York
April 22, 1897

T his menu cover contains a hard cardboard cover with three pages of light cardboard. A recessed beveled frame encases a portrait of General Porter, with the French and American flags with the insignia of the commandery appearing below. Each course of this meal is accompanied by a quote or poem having to do with France or Diplomacy. The last page is a history of General Porter's lifetime accomplishments.

BANQUET TO THE HONORABLE ARTILLERY COMPANY OF LONDON

Sponsored by the Ancient and Honorable Artillery
Company of Massachusetts
Symphony Hall
Boston, Massachusetts
October 5, 1903

This menu jacket is constructed of white leather with a silk inner lining. The menu has four pages, bound with a white ribbon. The first page shows an engraving of Boston with two hand-painted American flags with the Artillery Company flag between. There is also the raised seal of Boston and the date 1638. Page two represents the hand-painted seals of the two companies. Page three is the menu, and page four shows an engraving of London with two British flags and the artillery flag in between, with a silver shield, a red cross, and the date 1537.

SIXTEENTH ANNIVERSARY DINNER, COMPANY C ASSOCIATION

Sponsored by the Banquet Committee
Place Unknown
November 6, 1900

This light cardboard jacket features an engraving of the commander of the company. The inside front cover features another engraving of the featured speaker, Professor Alonzo Williams of Brown University. The menu is on the right fold, with the back cover listing all the company members.

COMPLIMENTARY DINNER TENDERED TO GEORGE PRESBURY ROWELL

The Waldorf Astoria
New York, New York
October 31, 1905

This distinctive menu contains a tribute to the honored guest— "He has lived three score years and lived them well. To be conscious of that, one need but know his enemies. Some are in high places. That demonstrates the courage of the man."

"Then here is to Rowell. If for every man to whom he has extended a helping hand, the powers will grant him a year of life. George Presbury Rowell will live forever."

TESTIMONIAL DINNER TO COLONEL H.O.S. HEISTAND

Sponsored by the Robert Fulton Monument Association
The Plaza Hotel
New York, New York
November 18, 1909

This menu consists of a light paper jacket housing five heavier paper pages. The cover is a reproduced signed photograph of colonel Heistand. The first page is printed in French, with the cocktails, wines and cigar brands in English. The next page lists the toasts; there were many luminaries at this dinner.

COMPLIMENTARY DINNER TO THOMAS A. HENDRICKS, VICE-PRESIDENT OF THE UNITED STATES

The Bay State Club
The Parker House, Boston, Massachusetts
Thursday, June 25th, 1885

The cover of this hard cardboard folder has an engraving of Thomas A. Hendricks on a round gild-edged, raised background. The Vice President has signed his name below the picture.

ANNUAL DINNER OF THE REPUBLICAN CLUB OF MASSACHUSETTS

Sponsored by the Republican Club
Symphony Hall
Boston, Massachusetts
Early 1900s

Portraits of Roosevelt and Fairbanks, the Republican candidates for the Presidency and Vice Presidency of the United States, grace the cover of this menu. The evening's speakers were three U.S. senators and the governor of Massachusetts.

SECOND ANNUAL DINNER, THE HOOKER ASSOCIATION OF MASSACHUSETTS

Sponsored by The Hooker Association
The American House
Boston, Massachusetts
November 13, 1907

This light cardboard cover showcases a black-and-white portrait of General Hooker. The four pages are bound by a red, white and blue ribbon. The inner pages feature a picture of General Hooker sitting atop Lookout Mountain, and a complete roster of all the members and officers of the Association.

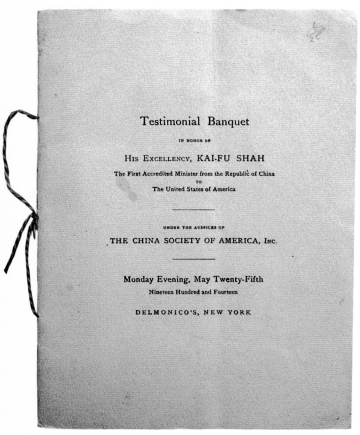

Testimonial Banquet

IN HONOR OF

HIS EXCELLENCY, KAI-FU SHAH

The First Accredited Minister from the Republic of China
TO
The United States of America

UNDER THE AUSPICES OF

THE CHINA SOCIETY OF AMERICA, INC.

Monday Evening, May Twenty-Fifth
Nineteen Hundred and Fourteen

DELMONICO'S, NEW YORK

DINNER TO THE GOVERNORS OF THE JEFFERSON FOUNDATION

Sponsored by the Jefferson Week Committee,
Thomas Jefferson
The Commodore
New York, New York
April 7, 1924

A brown-ink engraving of Jefferson's Monticello, adorns the jacket of this light cardboard menu. The interior consists of four pages: the first two list all members of the men's and women's committees, the third is the actual menu, while the last page details the program and the guests of honor. There are also three inserts: a proclamation from the governor of New York, a reproduction of a letter from the great, great grandson of Thomas Jefferson, and a list of boys nominated for the boy mayor's position in the Thomas Jefferson election.

TESTIMONIAL BANQUET IN HONOR OF HIS EXCELLENCY, KAI-FU SHAH, THE FIRST ACCREDITED MINISTER FROM THE REPUBLIC OF CHINA TO THE UNITED STATES OF AMERICA

Sponsored by The China Society of America, Inc.
Delmonico's
New York, New York
May 25, 1914

This simply designed menu is composed of a paper outer jacket and two folded inner pages, and bound with red string. The program and menu are printed in brown ink, with most of the pages taken up by the names of the guests and speakers. The title of one of the "special" guests was quite impressive (His Excellency, Frederico Alfonso Pezet, Envoy Extraordinary and Minister Plenipotentiary from Peru). This menu was written in French and Pall Mall cigarettes are listed along with the final course.

DINNER IN HONOUR OF
HIS EXCELLENCY PAUL W. CLAUDEL,
AMBASSADOR OF FRANCE

Sponsored by Assumption College, Worcester, Massachusetts
Bancroft Hotel
Worcester, Massachusetts
April 15, 1929

The menu jacket is of light cardboard and features the flags of the United States and France in red, white and blue with the portrait of the Ambassador in brown tones. The seal of Assumption College is at the top; the menu is bound with a red, white and blue tassel and contains two pages listing all guests. The menu is printed entirely in French.

ANNUAL DINNER OF THE INNER CIRCLE

Sponsored by the New York Shrine Inner Circle
Hotel Astor
New York, New York
February 9, 1924

This paper folder menu and program features on the cover a political cartoon introducing "Boom!Boom!" a rip-roaring revue by Norman Lynd. The entire menu represents a political satire, executed in black ink.

INAUGURAL DINNER IN HONOR OF HARRY S. TRUMAN, PRESIDENT OF THE UNITED STATES AND ALLEN W. BARKLEY, VICE PRESIDENT OF THE UNITED STATES

*Sponsored by the The Presidential Electors of
the United States*
The Mayflower
Washington, District of Columbia
January 19, 1949

This menu is composed of a light cardboard jacket with the great seal of the United States of America on the front. Seven interior pages include photos of the President and Vice President, the dinner programs, details of the seating of the Presidential table, an excerpt from the Constitution, and a complete list of all the Presidential electors. The detailed menu includes a salad named for the President's daughter and Martha Washington cake for dessert (prepared from the recipe of the Washington family). All the wines were a gift from the people of France. The cigars were a gift from the people of Cuba.

A LUNCHEON IN HONOR OF HIS MAJESTY THE KING OF THE HELLENES AND HER MAJESTY THE QUEEN OF THE HELLENES

Sponsored by the Mayor's Reception Committee,
the City of New York
The Waldorf-Astoria
New York, New York
November 2, 1953

The embossed cardboard cover, simply announces the luncheon with the seal of New York in blue at the lower righthand side. Inside, there are reproductions of the official state photographs of the King and Queen on pages two and three. The menu appears in English on the next page. The remaining pages detail the program, the Mayor's committee, the reception of guests and all the cooperating organizations.

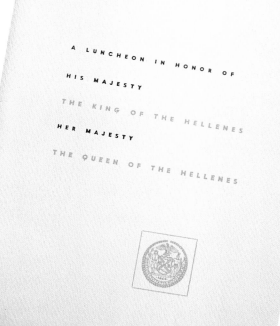

4TH
of
JULY

THE WENTWORTH BY THE SEA
PORTSMOUTH, N. H.

5

Cheers!

HOLIDAY

MENUS

*S*ince the dawn of man, celebrations of the seasonal changes have made life a little more exciting and pleasant. As we study history, we often read about great feasts that celebrated the rites of spring or the harvest's bounty. As we evolved and formal religious groups formed, Pagan festivals took on new meaning and eventually became the holidays we know today. Other holidays were dictated by the winning of great battles or some substantial event that changed the lives of the celebrants.

THE STUYVESANT HOTEL, HAPPY NEW YEAR DINNER 1914

Kingston, New York
December 31, 1913

Abeautiful woman dressed in the era's current style adorns this cover. Beauty and style were the key words on this special night, as this hotel offered the finest quality and greatest quantity of food. No less than 13 courses were set forth for this New Year's Eve.

THE CASTLE CLUB, NEW YEAR'S EVE DINNER 1924

Auburndale, Massachusetts
December 31, 1923

Atasteful yuletide bell and holly, with a seasonal Castle Club setting are featured on this cover. The private club offered a unique opportunity for those who wanted to spend this special night with the select few who shared their interests and social habits. The fare was elegant, but less ostentatious.

THE MANSION INN, NEW YEAR'S EVE FESTIVITIES 1925

Cochituate, Massachusetts
December 31, 1924

To look at this menu jacket you would think of a Christmas theme, but the insert welcomes you to a special New Year's dinner. There is a brief welcome from the Mansion Inn and a pleasant but unspectacular menu. On the bottom of the menu is the price per person: $8.00, indicating reservations were not required.

THE CHALFONTE-HADDON HALL, HAPPY NEW YEAR 1930

Atlantic City, New Jersey
January 1, 1930

A classic Father Time and Baby 1930 view the future through a golden telescope at this classic boardwalk resort hotel. This menu was prepared for a special New Year's Day meal; it offered many choices for those who came for the day or were spending the holiday away. On the inside front cover is a summer view of the hotel with the following poem—

"Here's a hearty wish to greet you,
Friendship and good fortune meet you,
And with the best of health unite
To make the coming New Year bright."

Terrace Garden
Wayland

1932

TERRACE GARDEN RESTAURANT,
ANNUAL FROLIC NEW YEAR'S EVE 1932
Wayland, Massachusetts
December 31, 1931

A Mardi-Gras theme adorns this cover, with a Baby 1932 floating down by parachute. This restaurant menu features Lobster Newburg and Filet Mignon with all the trimmings at $6.00 per person. (*Opposite*).

WASHINGTON'S BIRTHDAY

THE RIDGEWOOD, WASHINGTON'S BIRTHDAY DINNER

Daytona, Florida
February 22, 1904

This small menu is tastefully executed with portraits of George and Martha Washington displayed in gilded frames, with an eagle atop a globe of stars and stripes. The menu reflects the year round growing season with corn on the cob and fresh new peas served alongside traditional winter vegetables.

THE RIDGEWOOD, WASHINGTON'S BIRTHDAY DINNER

Daytona, Florida
February 22, 1918

The Ridgewood has taken on a whole new flamboyance with this year's menu. It boasts a gray and white cloud-like background with a gilded portrait of George Washington; below it a golden eagle is perched atop a real miniature thirteen starred flag. This menu jacket could be reused from year to year, as the insert is titled with the Ridgewood's coat of arms with the manager's name printed below. Of special note is the availability of many fresh fruits and vegetables.

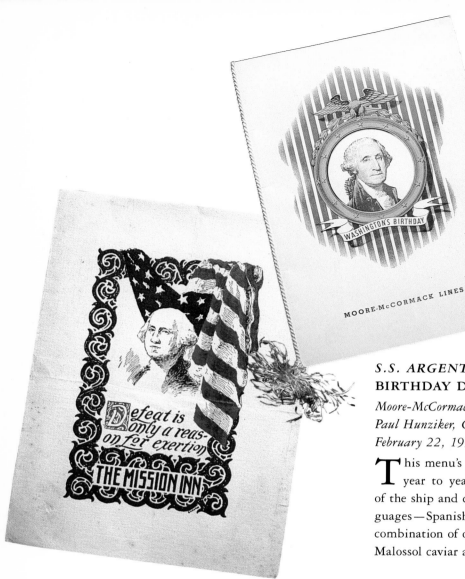

S.S. ARGENTINA, WASHINGTON'S BIRTHDAY DINNER

Moore-McCormack Lines
Paul Hunziker, Chef de Cuisine
February 22, 1950

This menu's jacket style allowed it to be reused from year to year. The insert is dated, with the names of the ship and chef. Entrees are printed in three languages—Spanish, French and English with an odd combination of offered foods including Beluga Malossol caviar and southern fried chicken.

THE MISSION INN, WASHINGTON'S BIRTHDAY DINNER

The Glenwood Mission Inn
Riverside, California
February 22, 1916

Patriotic is the key adjective for this cover. The back of the menu shows the mission's crest with the traditional mission bells.

The fare reflects classical California bounty with a slightly Spanish air. Many featured foods are California produce: navel oranges, fresh native lettuce, California cheese and olives. The presence of canned "Booth's" sardines reflects the taste of the chef or manager. This menu also lists many of the inn's special features including organ music at 1:30, 5 and 8 PM. There is even a curator's tour listed at 2:30 PM.

ABRAHAM LINCOLN'S BIRTHDAY

THE MIDDLESEX CLUB, LINCOLN NIGHT DINNER

Hotel Statler
Boston, Massachusetts
February 12, 1941

A gilded portrait of Lincoln set between a view of a log cabin and the White House graces this menu, thus pictorially showing the beginning and end of his life. This political evening lists the main speaker, the governor of Massachusetts, Leverett Saltonstall. The remaining attendees names read like the passenger list of the *Mayflower*. (*Opposite*).

MIDDLESEX CLUB

★

Lincoln
Night
Dinner

WEDNESDAY · FEBRUARY 12, 1941

ST. VALENTINE'S DAY

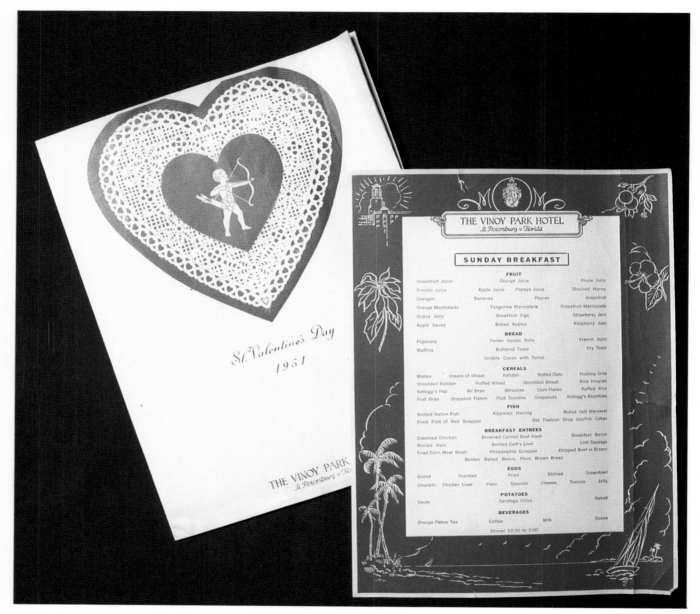

THE VINOY PARK HOTEL,
ST. VALENTINE'S DAY DINNER

St. Petersburg, Florida
February 14, 1951

This resort hotel offered standard fare with a few special additions, such as Sweetheart Salad and Orange Jello Hearts Delight, with whipped cream. There was also a special Valentine's dance with entertainment. An interesting item of note on the menu is Sanalac fat free milk.

ST. PATRICK'S DAY

THE POTTER HOTEL,
ST. PATRICK'S DAY DINNER

Santa Barbara, California
March 17, 1909

This lovely green menu jacket depicts a gilded singing harp with the name of St. Patrick on a bed of embossed clover. The "greening up" of the menu is accomplished by the addition of a creme de menthe punch.

EASTER

THE STUYVESANT, EASTER DINNER

Kingston, New York
1914

This tasseled jacket is highlighted by a Ben Austrian chick print. The menu content is quite standard with the addition of a few special Easter desserts.

THE FOURTH OF JULY

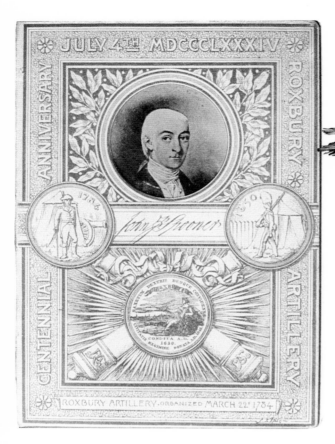

THE WENTWORTH BY THE SEA, FOURTH OF JULY DINNER MENU

Portsmouth, New Hampshire
July 4, 1923

This regionally famous resort overlooked the ocean and had as its logo a boy on a dolphin playing the flute. This menu represents the best in summer New England coastal resort dining.

ROXBURY CITY GUARD, CENTENNIAL ANNIVERSARY

Roxbury, Massachusetts
July 4, 1884

This classic menu is a beauty; the front and back of the hard board cover depicts the glorious history of the Roxbury Artillery, organized in March, 1784; the name was changed to the Roxbury City Guard in 1857. Their motto, "In Time of Peace Prepare for War" is featured prominently. The menu's fish course included boiled salmon and peas or lobster salad. Six meats were served in the main course, including various game birds. The desserts were quite special, and included seven varieties of cake, eight varieties of ice cream, fresh melon and bananas. The list of toasts required a minimum of 16 drinks.

THE BALSAMS, FOURTH OF JULY DINNER MENU

Dixville Notch, New Hampshire
July 4, 1941

This beautiful resort menu jacket depicts a boy and his grandfather ringing the liberty bell, with the caption "Ring! Grandpa, ring! Oh ring for liberty!" The rope the grandfather is pulling is a piece of gold cord. The bill of fare is replete with special dishes having patriotic names: Smithfield Ham, Lafayette, and Breast of Spring Chicken, Valley Forge. This menu does an excellent job representing the typical American Plan found at resort hotels of this period. This hotel still operates today. (*Opposite*).

Fourth of July

THE BALSAMS
DIXVILLE NOTCH, N. H.

THANKSGIVING

Thanksgiving is a holiday celebrated by one and all in the United States, that crosses over all lines of religion and national origin. Because of this, there are many versions of menus from all over the country.

BIGGS HOUSE, THANKSGIVING DAY DINNER

Portsmouth, Ohio
Thursday, November 25, 1875

This menu truly represents the bounty of the United States. Tasty temptations include fish from the sea and great lakes, 11 different styles of oysters, a game section including wild turkey, five varieties of native duck, wild boar, venison, black bear, squirrel and buffalo hump. The other menu selections include roasts, entrees, side dishes, boiled dishes, cold ornamental dishes, cold meats, relishes, vegetables, pastry, confectionery, fancy ornamental dishes, creams, jellies and desserts. The kitchen staff at this hotel must have been outstanding, if not prolific.

THE STUYVESANT, THANKSGIVING DINNER

Kingston, New York
November, 1914

A great deal of cost and effort has been put into this hotel's menu. It duly represents the region's bounty and the season's traditional fare.

THANKSGIVING POSTCARD

Mailed from a restaurant in Boston
Establishment Unknown
Boston, Massachusetts
November 26, 1919

The colorful embossed menu with a toast of thanks has a traditional postcard format on the back. Postage cost one cent.

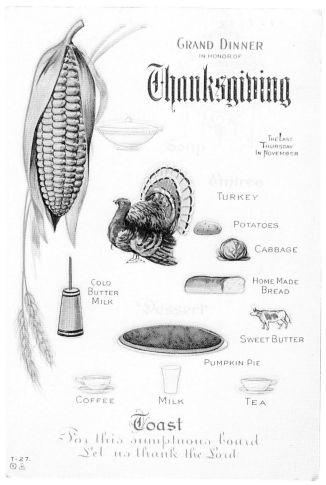

AMERICAN COLONY IN BERLIN, THANKSGIVING DAY DINNER

Hotel Kaiserhof
Berlin, Germany
Thursday, November 24, 1898

Being away from home at holiday time is a uniting force for people; this austere Thanksgiving menu served to bring our colony together. Venison was served alongside the traditional turkey, cranberry sauce, mince pie and vanilla ice cream. Also included are two pages of patriotic songs, with the final sing-along selection being "America." (*Opposite*).

THANKSGIVING TURKEY CARD

Advertising for Woods Boston Coffees
Boston, Massachusetts
Circa 1900

The turkey bravely states: "I only regret that I have but one life to give to my country."

U.S.S. NEW YORK,
THANKSGIVING DAY DINNER

Somewhere at port
Thursday, November 30, 1916

This traditional menu is not unlike what the military would serve today. This ship was at port because the band selections on the back of the menu contained many couple dances including the fox trot and waltz.

Thanksgiving 1926

HOTEL BRUNSWICK
BOSTON

HOTEL BRUNSWICK, THANKSGIVING DINNER

Boston, Massachusetts
Thursday, November 25, 1926

This menu cover is hand-painted. This hotel was one of many that offered a special complete dinner for a fixed price. Dinner was served from 12:00 to 8:30 PM and cost $3.50 per person and included grapefruit, soup, relishes, scallop Newburg, turkey or duck, six different vegetables, salad, dessert, cider and coffee.

HOTEL GREYSTONE, THANKSGIVING DINNER

New York, New York
Thursday, November 26, 1936

The pilgrims are prominently featured on this menu; often it is forgotten that they were the ones that celebrated the first Thanksgiving. This complete dinner served from 11:30 AM to 10:00 PM cost $1.25 per person.

Thanksgiving Greetings

THANKSGIVING DINNER
SERVED FROM 11:30 A. M. TO 10 P. M.
ONE DOLLAR TWENTY-FIVE
•

Imperial Fruit Cup   Blue Points on Half Shell
Cherrystone Clams, Neptune

Hearts of Celery
Rosebud Radishes   Queen Olives

Cream of Chicken, Dubarry
Chicken Broth, Mille Fonte

Roast Vermont Turkey, Old Fashioned Stuffing
Giblet Gravy   Cranberry Sauce
Roast Rack of Baby Lamb, Persiles, Fresh Mint Sauce
Roast Long Island Duckling, Apple Dressing

Mashed Turnips   Creamed White Onions
Brussels Sprouts
Mashed or Baked Potatoes
Sweet Potatoes, Louisville

Chef's Salad, Lorenza

English Plum Pudding with Hard Sauce
Hot Mince, Pumpkin or Apple Pie
Ice Cream, Assorted Cookies

Assorted Nuts and Raisins
Wayne County Cider

Demi Tasse

HOTEL GREYSTONE
THURSDAY, NOVEMBER 26, 1936

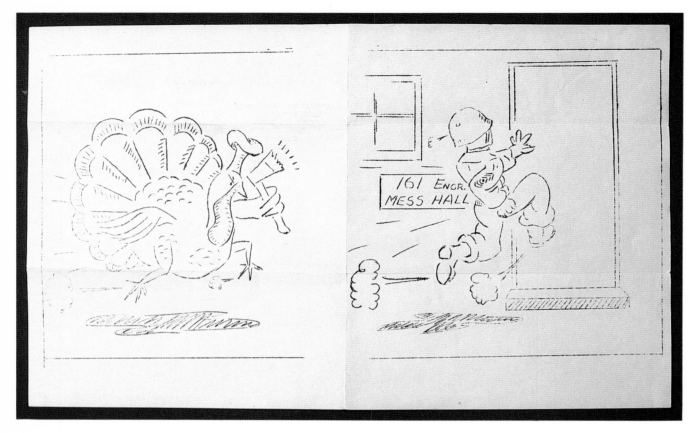

161 ENGINEERS MESS HALL,
THANKSGIVING DINNER

Location Unknown
Circa 1943

This mimeographed menu should be titled "The Turkey's Revenge." The menu contains traditional holiday fare that someone away from home would want for Thanksgiving Dinner.

SOMERSET HOTEL,
THANKSGIVING DINNER

Boston, Massachusetts
Thursday, November 27, 1958

This hotel was part of a larger corporation, and reflects the early corporate mentality that started advertising separate pricing for different menu items, including children's portions. The menu jacket shows the *Mayflower* and bountiful cornucopias with turkeys running in the wild. Over nine different colors are used to decorate this menu; many were hand tinted to impart an air of quality and elegance.

CHRISTMAS

Christmas is one of those special holidays that brings people back to their hearths and homes. But, not everyone can be home for the holidays. Some families have created the tradition of staying at a hotel or resort for the yuletide holiday, while some families move apart due to various reasons. But whatever the reason may be, the Christmas menu is one rich in decorative style and nostalgia.

THE NARRAGANSETT HOTEL, CHRISTMAS DINNER

Providence, Rhode Island
December 25, 1883

This menu is a classic; the outer jacket is covered in dark green velvet while the inner surface is printed on silk. The only decorative element is an embroidered white poinsettia. The menu features a 12 course dinner that begins with Blue Point oysters and flows through soups, hors d'oeuvres, salmon, filet of beef, quail, ribs of beef, turkey, vegetables, salad, sorbet, game, and dessert.

 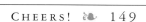

MERRY CHRISTMAS
DINING PLACEMARK MENU

Location and Establishment Unknown
Circa 1900

This tiny menu has an even smaller envelope pasted inside that contains the diner's name; it was most likely used as a seating place card.

THE STUYVESANT, CHRISTMAS DINNER

Kingston, New York
December 25, 1913

The illustration on this cover is titled "Making the Decision," referring probably to a holiday marriage engagement. The fare offered in the interior reflects the serious culinary commitment that this particular hotel made.

A Hearty Christmas Greeting
wishing you Health & Happiness
and all the
Compliments of the Season.

THE STUYVESANT, CHRISTMAS DINNER

Kingston, New York
December 25, 1915

"Christmas Chimes Recall Old Times" accents this simple but elegant picture of a bell and holly. The menu jacket is gaily embossed with poinsettias. The food listing is totally different from the 1913 version.

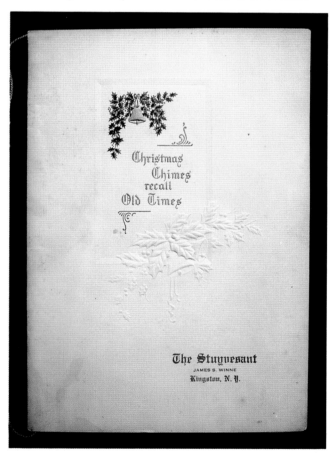

Christmas
Chimes
recall
Old Times

The Stuyvesant
JAMES S. WINNE
Kingston, N. Y.

HOTEL CANTERBURY, CHRISTMAS DINNER
BOSTON, MASSACHUSETTS
DECEMBER 25, 1925

This smaller resident hotel reflects a homestyle menu served from 1:00 to 3:00 PM. Some of the detail was hand-painted on this menu to further promote its "keepsake" appeal. The art work on the cover is by Edna M. Michard.

THE CAROLINA, CHRISTMAS DINNER

Pinehurst, North Carolina
December 25, 1928

This menu design evokes a warm, homey feeling. The photo is of Santa in someone's living room, even perhaps an area of the hotel. The opening of the fireplace has been hand-painted with watercolors to re-create the glow of a fire. The menu offers roast Carolina turkey or green gosling stuffed with potato.

THE UNITED STATES ARMED FORCES, CHRISTMAS DAY MEALS

Somewhere in Austria
December 25, 1945

This special military menu welcomes the first peace time Christmas in four years via a letter written by Gen. Mark W. Clark. The interior pictures many varieties of festive foods along with the complete day's menu, including breakfast, supper and dinner. The bottom fold of the menu is the full text of the General's Christmas wish for his troops.

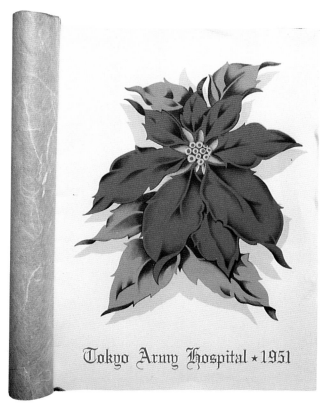

TOKYO ARMY HOSPITAL, CHRISTMAS DINNER

Tokyo, Japan
December 25, 1951

The poinsettia jacket of this Korean War menu contains eight pages including a picture of Col. Kenneth A. Brewer and his Christmas letter to his staff and troops. The menu is standard Christmas fare, but the remaining pages list every person involved with the hospital. The menu jacket has a protective parchment paper cover.

R.M.S. EDINBURGH CASTLE CHRISTMAS DINNER

Somewhere at Sea
December 25, 1959

This jacket was designed for all of the Union Castle shipping lines Christmas dinner menus. This particular menu was used in the first-class saloon of the *Edinburgh Castle*. The spelling of "saloon" is as it appears on the menu.

DINNER TO THE HONORABLE
CHARLES·E·HUGHES
ASSOCIATE JUSTICE OF THE
SUPREME COURT OF THE UNITED STATES
BY THE
LOTOS·CLUB
NEW YORK

MENU · MEDIUM MUMFORD COVES
CLEAR GREEN TURTLE
SWEETBREAD TIMBALES · SUPREME
ESCALLOPES OF STRIPED BASS · DIPLOMATIC
BEEF TENDERLOIN · WASHINGTON
AMERICAN SHERBET
REDHEAD DUCK · CELERY SALAD
STRAWBERRY MOUSSE · PETIT FOURS
ROQUEFORT & CAMEMBERT CHEESE
COFFEE · ·

· NOVEMBER XIX · MCMX ·

SINDELAR

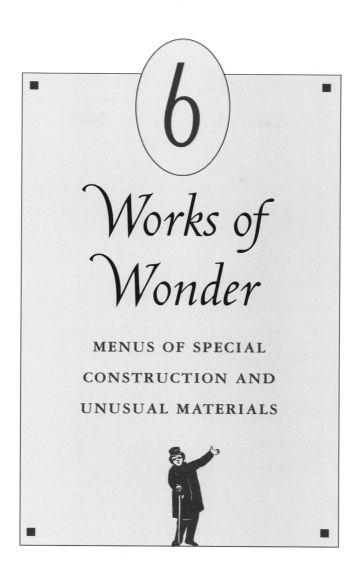

6

Works of Wonder

MENUS OF SPECIAL CONSTRUCTION AND UNUSUAL MATERIALS

*M*enu design and construction can sometimes take very non-traditional directions. Whether it be in size, materials, construction, shape or print design, they surprise, delight and amaze.

DINNER TO WALTER CAMP

Sponsored by the graduates of Yale University
Concert Hall, Madison Square Garden
New York, New York
February 26, 1892

The front and back cover of this menu are made of pigskin, and formed into the shape of a football; the four inner pages are laced with brown cord. The menu and accompanying song book commemorate Walter Camp's contributions to Yale and the world of sports. Walter Camp is heralded as the "Father of football."

THE ICE MENS' 33RD ANNUAL BALL

Sponsored by the Employees of the Boston Ice Company
Mechanic Building, Grand Hall
Boston, Massachusetts
November 15, 1899

The jacket of this menu is of heavy crepe paper, with an appliqued piece of plastic parchment decorated with tiny silk bows at each corner. The center of the cover is a die cut shield on a bed of silk; a tiny bronze plaque proclaims "How would you like to be the Iceman?" Attached to this is a miniature pair of bronze ice tongs gripping a small block of glass "ice." This is indeed a masterpiece. (*Opposite*).

THE SECOND ANNUAL BANQUET

Sponsored by the Rochester Board of Trade
Hotel Wrisley
Rochester, New York
March 23, 1894

The jacket consists of heavy waxed parchment, which has been heated at the edges to cause it to crinkle. The top right corner is bent forward and tied with a silk ribbon. The pastoral mountain scene is secured to the front by two silk bows. The interior of the menu is surprisingly mundane, including the dinner fare.

ICE MENS'BALL

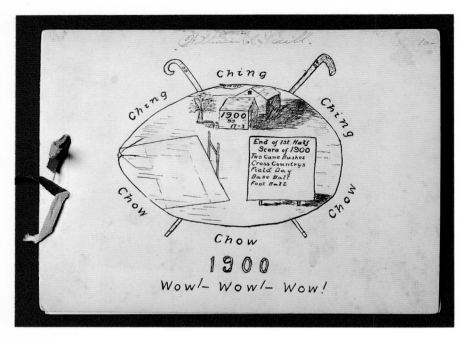

CHING, CHING, CHING—
CHOW, CHOW, CHOW—1900—
WOW—WOW—WOW

Sponsored by an Unknown: fraternity or Class Dinner, the
Class of 1901 (the College may be Harvard)
The Bay State Club
Boston, Massachusetts
November 1, 1898

Hand designed on light cardboard, the entire menu is
full of cartoons created for this evening. The boards
are tied with grey and purple ribbon.

ELEVENTH ANNUAL MEETING AND
BANQUET

Sponsored by the Society of the War of 1812, in the
Commonwealth of Massachusetts
The Copley Square Hotel
Boston, Massachusetts
January 10, 1905

This jacket is hand crafted of heavy paper; the edges
have been scalloped to look like waves. The ship re-
sembles the *Constitution,* and is hand-painted. The interior menu is typeset in a traditional manner.

THE CARAVAN OF ALLEPPO
DINNER AND INITIATION

Sponsored by the Alleppo Temple,
Nobles of the Mystic Shrine
Mechanics Hall
Boston, Massachusetts
May 29, 1911

This menu would scare anyone; interested in member-ship? It is 8 inches × 10 inches folded, and accordions out four times. The front tells its own story, while the back lists the members and quotes bits of shrine wisdom. The menu begins with yellow mill pond trunk sewer oysters in the ¾ shell, and continues with additions like gutter snipe, sea spiders with mayonnaise, skunk stuffed with poultice and bald mice pie to mention but a few of the tempting tidbits offered.

CARNIVAL AND BALL

Sponsored by the Crew of the U.S.S Salem
Somewhere at Sea
June 27, 1919

The cover design of this paper menu is reproduced from a painting by Mrs. R.E.L. Kincaid-Turner. The interior consists of three, centerfolded sheets. Reproductions of the *U.S.S. Salem* and a portrait of the commanding officer, Captain Hayne Ellis, U.S.N. are included. The remaining pages are the menu, program of events and the Ship's roster.

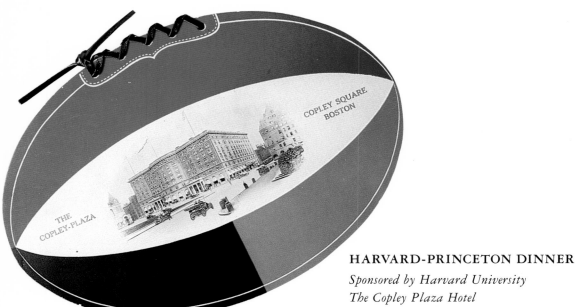

HARVARD-PRINCETON DINNER

Sponsored by Harvard University
The Copley Plaza Hotel
Boston, Massachusetts
November 6, 1926

This die-cut menu is in the shape of a football. The covers are light cardboard with three paper inner pages, secured at the top with a leather thong. One of the pages lists all team members for both Universities and the support staffs. Each page is printed in three colors, while the cover is printed in four, with an engraving of the Copley Plaza Hotel.

100TH ANNIVERSARY DINNER

Sponsored by The Atlantic National Bank of Boston
Hotel Statler
Boston, Massachusetts
April 17, 1928

These menu covers were all handmade; the material is heavy tissue paper quarter-folded to form the jacket; there is a gilded pattern throughout the paper design. The sailing ship (the original charter) engraving is affixed to the cover with black corner miters. The printed inner pages are tied to the jacket with a blue silk ribbon. The evening's music was provided by the Atlantic National Bank Band, and there were seventy tables of ten persons each in attendance.

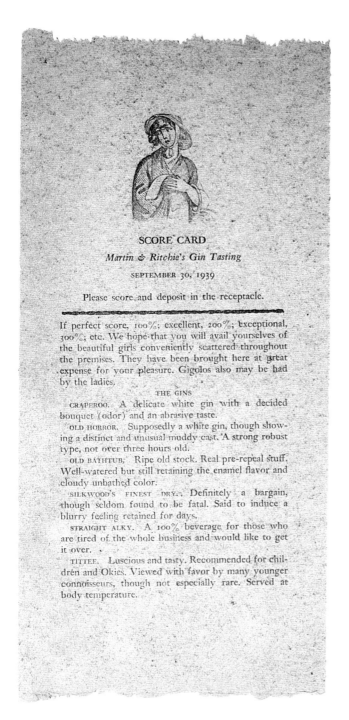

SCORE CARD

Martin & Ritchie's Gin Tasting

SEPTEMBER 30, 1939

Please score and deposit in the receptacle.

If perfect score, 100%; excellent, 200%; exceptional, 300%; etc. We hope that you will avail yourselves of the beautiful girls conveniently scattered throughout the premises. They have been brought here at great expense for your pleasure. Gigolos also may be had by the ladies.

THE GINS

CRAPEROO. A delicate white gin with a decided bouquet (odor) and an abrasive taste.

OLD HORROR. Supposedly a white gin, though showing a distinct and unusual muddy cast. A strong robust type, not over three hours old.

OLD BATHTUB. Ripe old stock. Real pre-repeal stuff. Well-watered but still retaining the enamel flavor and cloudy unbathed color.

SILKWOOD'S FINEST DRY. Definitely a bargain, though seldom found to be fatal. Said to induce a blurry feeling retained for days.

STRAIGHT ALKY. A 100% beverage for those who are tired of the whole business and would like to get it over.

TITTEE. Luscious and tasty. Recommended for children and Okies. Viewed with favor by many younger connoisseurs, though not especially rare. Served at body temperature.

BOHEMIAN NIGHT

Sponsored by Wannamoisett Country Club
The Wannamoisett Country Club
Location Unknown
Exact Date Unknown (probably 1930s)

This poster promises everything Bohemia has to offer. A Bohemian supper served by Bohemians, a Bohemian orchestra and the famous Terpsichorean artists, the Worths.

SCORE CARD MENU

Sponsored by Martin & Ritchie's Gin Tasting
Location Unknown
September 30, 1939

This menu speaks for itself. It is printed on toilet tissue with the suggestion "that you score the gin and deposit in the receptacle."

THE DIE-CUT MENU

The concept of restaurant menus with different shapes started to pro-liferate in the late 1930s and early 1940s and made great souvenirs. The fanciful shapes highlighted special features of the restaurant or capitalized on the importance of nearby landmarks and places of interest.

THE SALAD BOWL

Filene's Department Store
Boston, Massachusetts
August 29, 1940

This salad bowl was a fresh concept at the time, and offered the weary shopper a creative, light lunch. No tipping was allowed at this restaurant.

CUPID'S INN

Springfield, Massachusetts and Holyoke, Massachusetts
Circa 1938–1940

These restaurants never closed; you could get a Cupid's special hamburger for 15 cents and a cup of coffee for a nickel. The restaurant's name is highly appropriate, everyone loved the prices.

THE COVERED WAGON

Somewhere in Minnesota
August 4, 1941

This is a great menu "coming and going." It offered great steaks and a major wine and beverage list. The covered wagon giant Porterhouse steak for two with a complete dinner cost $3.00. Two boiled lamb chops or rare prime rib complete dinners cost $1.00. The only problem was that the address of the restaurant did not appear on the menu.

THE BIG TREE INN

Des Moines Highway
Des Moines, Iowa
Circa 1940

The restaurant history appears on the back of the menu. The building was constructed for the Panama Pacific International Exposition held at San Francisco in 1915 and was built from a giant Redwood tree approximately 2500 years old; somehow, it got to Des Moines. Fried chicken and sandwiches were the big featured items.

GULF PIER CAFE

Galveston, Texas
Circa 1940

This must be a seafood restaurant, a picture of the Gulf Pier Cafe appears on the back of this menu. They were "famous" for their stuffed flounder dinner at one dollar.

PANCAKES

Deerfield Beach, Florida
1948–1949 Season

Home of the famous pancake, this restaurant called its diners "pancakers." Their hours were interesting: 8:00 AM to 2:50 PM and 5:00 PM to 8:20 PM. Did they have soaps back then?

HOT SHOPPES KIDDIES' MENU

Location Unknown
August 7, 1951

Kids were starting to become big business and more restaurants were beginning to cater to them with special, cute menus.

ROD'S STEAK HOUSE
Williams, Arizona
Circa 1950s

"The Gateway to the Grand Canyon" was proud of their meat and Rod warned you not to order it well done. Additionally, Rod noted that the little steer bears the same brand as your steak.

THE LITTLE BROWN JUG
The Little Brown Hotel
Julesburg, Colorado
Circa 1950s

Julesburg was once known as the "Wickedest City in the West" according to the inner cover of this little brown jug menu.

DINNER TO ROBLEY D. SHANS
REAR ADMIRAL U.S.N.
The Lotos Club
New York, New York
November 2, 1907

The cover of this menu is decorated with an intricately designed anchor. The menu incorporates all of the ships Shans sailed or commanded, along with his portrait and life's accomplishments. (*Opposite*).

THE LOTOS CLUB; SPECIAL DESIGN

Every once in a while a collector stumbles onto a special find. The Lotos Club is one of the oldest literary clubs in the United States and was founded on March 15, 1870 by a group of young writers, journalists and critics. An early club member, Samuel L. Clemens (Mark Twain) called it "The Ace of Clubs." One of the club's oldest traditions is to hold what they still call "State Dinners." In earlier days magnificent engraved formal menus were created that depicted in fine detail the life's accomplishments of the person being honored. Through these menus, designed by Thomas A. Sindelar, an appreciation of the Lotos Club's infinite sense of style and fellowship can be gained. The menus are extremely large, with the average size being 12½ inches × 17 inches, not including the covers.

The author thanks the current management of the Lotos Club who were kind enough to share their history. The Lotos Club exists today in New York City.

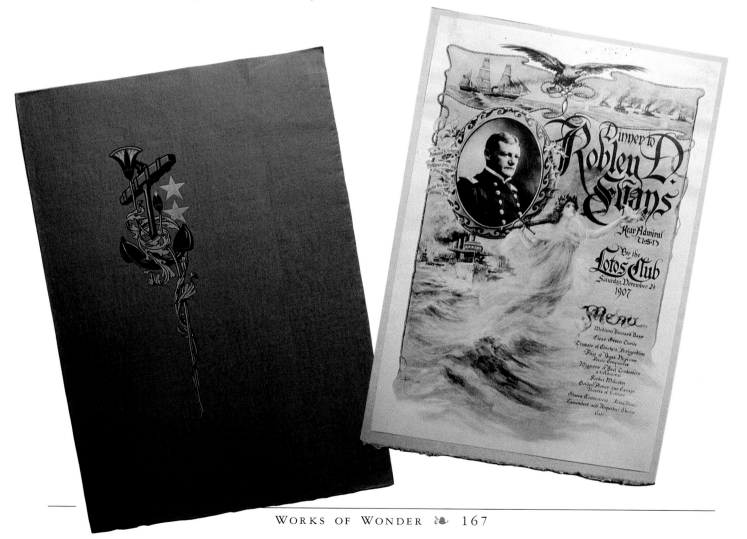

DINNER TO THE HONORABLE CHARLES E. HUGHES, ASSOCIATE JUSTICE OF THE SUPREME COURT OF THE UNITED STATES

The Lotos Club
New York, New York
November 19, 1910

The cover is folded heavy gray paper board, while the menu is glued to a black mat. Pictured is "Justice" holding the ubiquitous scales and an olive branch; she is wrapped in Old Glory. Alongside the engraving, a beautifully framed portrait of the associate justice appears.

DINNER TO THE HONORABLE MAHLON PITNEY, ASSOCIATE JUSTICE OF THE SUPREME COURT OF THE UNITED STATES

The Lotos Club
New York, New York
May 2, 1912

A Lotos flower is featured on the cover, with the seal of the United States in the center. Reproduced on a cream-colored frame mat, the menu features a portrait along with a visioned justice with scale and sword. The American Eagle stands upon a seal and the personal history of the Associate Justice is printed alongside.

DINNER TO MAURICE MAETERLINCK

The Lotos Club
New York, New York
January 3, 1920

A simple blue cover frames the engraved menu honoring this famed Belgian playwright, winner of the Nobel Prize for Literature; the engraving depicts many of the characters from Maeterlinck's famous works. This menu is signed by the artist Thomas A. Sindelar.

DINNER TO JOHN ELDERKIN

The Lotos Club
New York, New York
February 22, 1921

Housed in a lovely green cover, this menu is dedicated to one of the original founders of the Lotos Club, and is in celebration of his eightieth birthday.

DINNER TO MARY GARDEN

The Lotos Club
New York, New York
January 29, 1922

Housed in a white cover, this menu is dedicated to one of the world's most famous sopranos and features her portrait surrounded by her impressive roles with an inset of her first character role. In later years, Mary Garden became the director of the Chicago Opera Company.

SAMPLES

··· OF ···

BALL ORDERS, MENUS, WEDDING CABINETS, Etc.

CARTER, RICE & CO. (CORPORATION),

1892-93.   BOSTON, MASS.

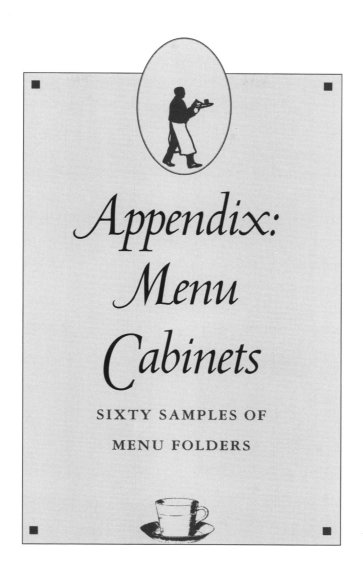

Appendix: Menu Cabinets

SIXTY SAMPLES OF
MENU FOLDERS

*T*he sample book featured in this chapter was circulated and used one hundred years ago by restaurants, hotels, caterers and event planners who did not have the time or inclination to create a personalized menu jacket design for every event. These cabinets found their way into every manner of establishment and manifested every aspect of daily life: from the four seasons with holidays and festivals to patriotic scenes embodying a specific era and the growth of national pride. They depict professions, social and fraternal organizations, and a wide variety of natural scenes. The significance of these cabinets in their original form cannot be quantified, as they represent the period's need for mass-produced concepts that had to be able to be individualized as the ever-increasing number of events, restaurants and hotels required expedient and cost-effective menu production. Thus, the menu cabinet was born.

Sample book cover: Carter, Rice & Company 1892-1893 Boston, Massachusetts, Ball Orders, Menus, Wedding Cabinets, etc.

Each cabinet was numbered and a price was given per hundred and per thousand. The inside of the cover had the price list and ordering information attached. Many of these folders could be purchased painted, or the buyer had the option of painting them himself.

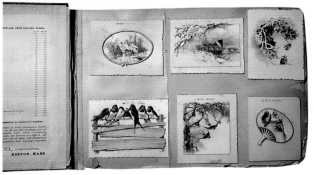

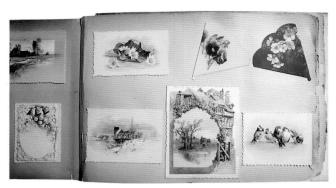

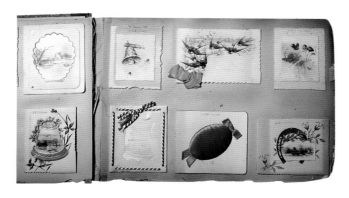

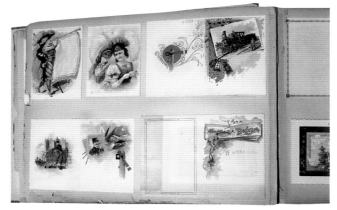

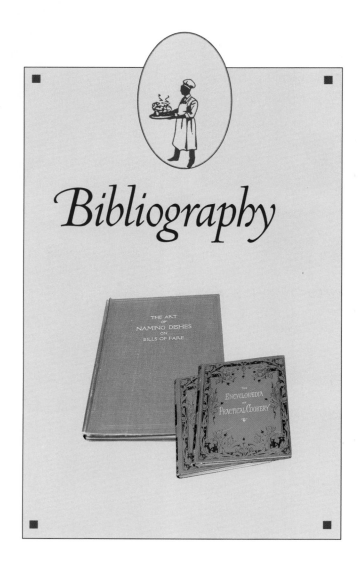

Bibliography

A s I began my collecting experience I was often challenged by the thought of how difficult it is to create a special events menu, to design a traditional hotel menu, or produce a restaurant bill of fare. Today, as I work with clients, I must draw upon collective creative juices and the resources that are within my reach. The thought occurred to me what might the chefs and catering managers of the 1800s and early 1900s have used to develop ideas and menu formats.